THE ENCYCLOPEDIA OF PSYCHOACTIVE DRUGS

IN 25 VOLUMES
Each title on a specific drug or drug-related problem

MUSHROOMS

THE ENCYCLOPEDIA OF PSYCHOACTIVE DRUGS

MUSHROOMS

Psychedelic Fungi

PETER E. FURST, Ph.D.

State University of New York
Harvard University

1986
CHELSEA HOUSE PUBLISHERS
NEW YORK
NEW HAVEN   PHILADELPHIA

SENIOR EDITOR: William P. Hansen
ASSOCIATE EDITORS: John Haney, Richard S. Mandell
ASSISTANT EDITOR: Paula Edelson
CAPTIONS: Marshall N. Levin
EDITORIAL COORDINATOR: Karyn Gullen Browne
ART DIRECTOR: Susan Lusk
ART COORDINATOR: Carol McDougall
LAYOUT: Ghila Krajzman, Tenaz Mehta
ART ASSISTANTS: Noreen M. Lamb, Victoria Tomaselli
PICTURE RESEARCH: Ian Ensign
COVER PHOTO: Peter E. Furst

First Printing

Library of Congress Cataloging in Publication Data
Furst, Peter E.
   Mushrooms, psychedelic fungi.

   (The Encyclopedia of psychoactive drugs)
   Bibliography; p.
   Includes index.
   Summary: Examines the uses and hallucinogenic properties of psychedelic
mushrooms, one of nature's oldest and most misunderstood drugs.
      1. Mushrooms, Hallucinogenic—Juvenile literature. [1. Mushrooms,
Hallucinogenic. 2. Drugs] I. Title. II. Series.
QK617.F94 1986   615'.7883   85-17522
ISBN 0-87754-767-X

Chelsea House Publishers

Harold Steinberg, Chairman & Publisher
Susan Lusk, Vice President
A Division of Chelsea House Educational Communications, Inc.

Chelsea House Publishers
133 Christopher Street
New York, NY 10014

Photos courtesy of American Museum of Natural History; Heather Angel/Biofotos;
AP/Wide World Photos; The Bettmann Archive; Peter Furst; Harvard University
Botanical Museum (R. Gordon Wasson Collection); Marshall Cavendish, Ltd.;
McGraw-Hill Publishers; Museum of the Amerian Indian; Western Publishing, Inc.

CONTENTS

The fly agaric, Amanita muscaria, *used by Siberian shamans and North American Indians, was the first fungi known to be psychoactive.*

FOREWORD

In the Mainstream of American Life

The rapid growth of drug use and abuse is one of the most dramatic changes in the fabric of American society in the last 20 years. The United States has the highest level of psychoactive drug use of any industrialized society. It is 10 to 30 times greater than it was 20 years ago.

According to a recent Gallup poll, young people consider drugs the leading problem that they face. One of the legacies of the social upheaval of the 1960s is that psychoactive drugs have become part of the mainstream of American life. Schools, homes, and communities cannot be "drug proofed." There is a demand for drugs—and the supply is plentiful. Social norms have changed and drugs are not only available—they are everywhere.

Almost all drug use begins in the preteen and teenage years. These years are few in the total life cycle, but critical in the maturation process. During these years adolescents face the difficult tasks of discovering their identity, clarifying their sexual roles, asserting their independence, learning to cope with authority, and searching for goals that will give their lives meaning. During this intense period of growth, conflict is inevitable and the temptation to use drugs is great. Drugs are readily available, adolescents are curious and vulnerable, there is peer pressure to experiment, and there is the temptation to escape from conflicts.

No matter what their age or socioeconomic status, no group is immune to the allure and effects of psychoactive drugs. The U.S. Surgeon General's report, "Healthy People," indicates that 30% of all deaths in the United States

A drawing of a 1,200-year-old Mexican clay sculpture of a goddess or priestess drumming on a large mushroom effigy.

are premature because of alcohol and tobacco use. However, the most shocking development in this report is that mortality in the age group between 15 and 24 has increased since 1960 despite the fact that death rates for all other age groups have declined in the 20th century. Accidents, suicides, and homicides are the leading cause of death in young people 15 to 24 years of age. In many cases the deaths are directly related to drug use.

THE ENCYCLOPEDIA OF PSYCHOACTIVE DRUGS answers the questions that young people are likely to ask about drugs, as well as those they might not think to ask, but should. Topics include: what it means to be intoxicated; how drugs affect mood; why people take drugs; who takes them; when they take them; and how much they take. They will learn what happens to a drug when it enters the body. They will learn what it means to get "hooked" and how it happens. They will learn how drugs affect their driving, their school work, and those around them—their peers, their family, their friends, and their employers. They will learn what the signs are that indicate that a friend or a family member may have a drug problem and to identify four stages leading from drug use to drug abuse. Myths about drugs are dispelled.

National surveys indicate that students are eager for information about drugs and that they respond to it. Students not only need information about drugs—they want information. How they get it often proves crucial. Providing young people with accurate knowledge about drugs is one of the most critical aspects.

THE ENCYCLOPEDIA OF PSYCHOACTIVE DRUGS synthesizes the wealth of new information in this field and demystifies this complex and important subject. Each volume in the series is written by an expert in the field. Handsomely illustrated, this multi-volume series is geared for teenage readers. Young people will read these books, share them, talk about them, and make more informed decisions because of them.

Miriam Cohen, Ph.D.
Contributing Editor

A Yakut shaman in ceremonial dress. People from this mushroom-eating tribe of northern Siberia were first studied less than 90 years ago.

INTRODUCTION

The Gift of Wizardry
Use and Abuse

JACK H. MENDELSON, M.D.
NANCY K. MELLO, PH.D.
Alcohol and Drug Abuse Research Center
Harvard Medical School—McLean Hospital

Dorothy to the Wizard:

"I think you are a very bad man," said Dorothy.
"Oh, no, my dear; I'm really a very good man; but I'm a very bad Wizard."
—from THE WIZARD OF OZ

Man is endowed with the gift of wizardry, a talent for discovery and invention. The discovery and invention of substances that change the way we feel and behave are among man's special accomplishments, and like so many other products of our wizardry, these substances have the capacity to harm as well as to help. The substance itself is neutral, an intricate molecular structure. Yet, "too much" can be sickening, even deadly. It is man who decides how each substance is used, and it is man's beliefs and perceptions that give this neutral substance the attributes to heal or destroy.

Consider alcohol—available to all and yet regarded with intense ambivalence from biblical times to the present day. The use of alcoholic beverages dates back to our earliest ancestors. Alcohol use and misuse became associated with the worship of gods and demons. One of the most powerful Greek gods was Dionysus, lord of fruitfulness and god of wine. The Romans adopted Dionysus but changed his name to Bacchus. Festivals and holidays associated with Bacchus celebrated the harvest and the origins of life. Time has blurred the images of the Bacchanalian festival, but the theme of drunkenness as a major part of celebration has survived the pagan gods and remains a familiar part of modern society. The term "Bacchanalian festival" conveys a more appealing image than "drunken orgy" or "pot party," but whatever the label, some of the celebrants will inevitably start up the "high" escalator to the next plateau. Once there, the de-escalation is difficult for many.

According to reliable estimates, one out of every ten 10% Americans develops a serious alcohol-related problem sometime in his or her lifetime. In addition, automobile accidents caused by drunken drivers claim the lives of tens of thousands every year. Many of the victims are gifted young people, just starting out in adult life. Hospital emergency rooms abound with patients seeking help for alcohol-related injuries.

Who is to blame? Can we blame the many manufacturers who produce such an amazing variety of alcoholic beverages? Should we blame the educators who fail to explain the perils of intoxication, or so exaggerate the dangers of drinking that no one could possibly believe them? Are friends to blame—those peers who urge others to "drink more and faster," or the macho types who stress the importance of being able to "hold your liquor"? Casting blame, however, is hardly constructive, and pointing the finger is a fruitless way to deal with problems. Alcoholism and drug abuse have few culprits but many victims. Accountability begins with each of us, every time we choose to use or to misuse an intoxicating substance.

It is ironic that some of man's earliest medicines, derived from natural plant products, are used today to poison and to intoxicate. Relief from pain and suffering is one of society's many continuing goals. Over 3,000 years ago, the Therapeutic Papyrus of Thebes, one of our earliest written records, gave instructions for the use of opium in the treatment of pain. Opium, in the form of its major derivative, morphine, remains one of the most powerful drugs we have for pain relief. But opium, morphine, and similar compounds, such as heroin, have also been used by many to induce changes in mood and feeling. Another example of man's misuse of a natural substance is the coca leaf, which for centuries was used by the Indians of Peru to reduce fatigue and hunger. Its modern derivative, cocaine, lidocaine? has important medical use as a local anesthetic. Unfortunately, its increasing abuse in the 1980s has reached epidemic proportions.

The purpose of this series is to provide information about the nature and behavioral effects of alcohol and drugs, and the probable consequences of both their moderate use and abuse. The authors believe that up-to-date, objective information about alcohol and drugs will help readers make better decisions as to whether to use them or not. The information presented here (and in other books in this series) is based on many clinical and laboratory studies and observations by people from diverse walks of life.

Over the centuries, novelists, poets, and dramatists have provided us with many insights into the beneficial and problematic aspects of alcohol and drug use. Physicians, lawyers, biologists, psychologists, and social scientists have contributed to a better understanding of the causes and consequences of using these substances. The authors in this series have attempted to gather and condense all the latest information about drug use and abuse. They have also described the sometimes wide gaps in our knowledge and have suggested some new ways to answer many difficult questions.

One such question, for example, is how do alcohol and drug problems get started? And what is the best way to treat them when they do? Not too many years ago, alcoholics and drug abusers were regarded as evil, immoral, or both. It is now recognized that these persons suffer from very complicated diseases involving deep psychological and social problems. To understand how the disease begins and progresses, it is necessary to understand the nature of the substance, the behavior of the afflicted person, and the characteristics of the society or culture in which he lives.

The diagram below shows the interaction of these three factors. The arrows indicate that the substance not only affects the user personally, but the society as well. Society influences attitudes towards the substance, which in turn affect its availability. The substance's impact upon the society may support or discourage the use and abuse of that substance.

SUBSTANCE
(ALCOHOL OR DRUG)

PERSON ←――――――→ SOCIETY

The Greek biographer Plutarch, who lived from 46 to 119, believed that mushrooms were generated by lightning bolts.

Although many of the social environments we live in are very similar, some of the most subtle differences can strongly influence our thinking and behavior. Where we live, go to school and work, whom we discuss things with—all influence our opinions about drug use and misuse. Yet we also share certain commonly accepted beliefs that outweigh any differences in our attitudes. The authors in this series have tried to identify and discuss the central, most crucial issues concerning drug use and misuse.

Regrettably, man's wizardry in developing new substances in medical therapeutics has not always been paralleled by intelligent usage. Although we do know a great deal about the effects of alcohol and drugs, we have yet to learn how to impart that knowledge, especially to young adults.

Does it matter? What harm does it do to smoke a little pot or have a few beers? What is it like to be intoxicated? How long does it last? Will it make me feel really fine? Will it make me sick? What are the risks? These are but a few of the questions answered in this series, which, hopefully, will enable the reader to make wise decisions concerning the crucial issue of drugs.

Information sensibly acted upon can go a long way towards helping everyone develop his or her best self. As one keen and sensitive observer, Dr. Lewis Thomas, has said,

> *"There is nothing at all absurd about the human condition. We. matter. It seems to me a good guess, hazarded by a good many people who have thought about it, that we may be engaged in the formation of something like a mind for the life of this planet. If this is so, we are still at the most primitive stage, still fumbling with language and thinking, but infinitely capacitated for the future. Looked at this way, it is remarkable that we've come as far as we have in so short a period, really no time at all as geologists measure time. We are the newest, the youngest, and the brightest thing around."*

This clay figurine, which is about 2000 years old, is from Colima, Mexico, and depicts four men dancing around an oversized mushroom. The knob in the center of the cap identifies the mushroom as being of the genus Psilocybe, *a type of fungi used by Mexican Indians and known to have psychedelic, or mind-altering, effects.*

CHAPTER 1

THE WORLD OF THE FUNGI

Of the nearly 6,000 identified species of mushrooms, less than 2% are known to be hallucinogenic, or able to produce perceptions not based on reality. And only a fraction of these have been used for this purpose. Though there is considerable evidence for a wider use of these fungi in ancient times, only in a few parts of the world have hallucinogenic mushrooms continued to play a role in recent times.

Many people consider these mushrooms toxic, or capable of causing damage to the body, but research has not shown that they cause permanent or even temporary physiological damage. Unlike drugs such as heroin and nicotine, they are not addictive. What psychedelic mushrooms do, rather, is act on the central nervous system in ways that temporarily alter visual or auditory perceptions, sometimes to extraordinary degrees. A Mexican Indian, drawing from his rich mythological world, claimed that, "the little mushroom spirits are the spirits of the Holy Earth. They take me to the ancestors, they speak with the voice of God, they show me my life. And if I ask them why this man or this woman is ill, or whatever it is one wishes to know, the mushroom spirits will tell me."

Outside their traditional cultural setting, however, mushroom use can be hazardous. Experimentation with wild mushrooms by inexperienced and unknowledgable people can have serious consequences. Also, hallucinogenic mushrooms sold on the black market are more often than not ordinary edible species treated with potentially dangerous substances. For these reasons, though there is little evidence that mushrooms pose a threat to one's health, federal law prohibits possession or use of the most commonly used hallucinogenic species.

To appreciate what psychoactive mushrooms are, how they affect the body, and the roles they play, or have played, in religion, myth, and medicine, one has to understand the biology of fungi—the group of organisms that includes mushrooms, puffballs, and toadstools. For over two thousand years, since the time of the Greek philosopher Theophrastus (372–287 B.C.E.), often called the "father of biology," the fungi were grouped with green plants in a single kingdom.

Huichol Indians in Nayarit, Mexico, preparing to celebrate a squash festival. Many indigenous peoples in all parts of the world relate religious practices to the plants that sustain them. A Mexican adage maintains that " whatever it is one wishes to know, the mushroom spirits will tell."

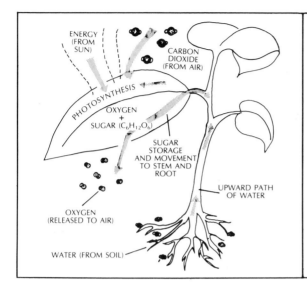

ENERGY
(FROM
SUN)

CARBON
DIOXIDE
(FROM AIR)

PHOTOSYNTHESIS

OXYGEN
+
SUGAR ($C_6H_{12}O_6$)

SUGAR
STORAGE
AND MOVEMENT
TO STEM AND
ROOT

UPWARD PATH
OF WATER

OXYGEN
(RELEASED TO AIR)

WATER (FROM SOIL)

Figure 1. *During photosynthesis, sunlight is the source of energy by which carbon dioxide (CO_2) and water (H_2O) combine, releasing oxygen (O_2) into the air and forming sugars ($C_6H_{12}O_6$), the basic food for all animal life.*

Today they are classified with molds, mildews, and yeasts in a separate kingdom, independent of the plant and animal kingdoms.

Green plants, employing a process known as photosynthesis, use sunlight to produce simple and complex sugars. The fundamental producers of food for all animals, green plants have often been considered the beginning and end of all life. But as decomposers of the environment, the fungi are no less essential. It is the fungi that, by consuming waste matter, return carbon dioxide to the atmosphere and nutrients to the soil, thereby providing substances necessary for the growth of vegetation.

Even when fungi were included with green plants in the plant kingdom, people had trouble deciding just what they were, how they reproduced, and where they belonged in the mosaic of life. In the 1st century C.E. Plutarch thought that the truffle, a tuberous fungus prized by epicureans, was generated by thunder and lightning. A respected 17th-century biologist even proposed that the truffle sprang from the semen of rutting deer! Sixteenth-century herbalists argued that fungi were intermediate between animate and inanimate nature, or were "superfluous moisture" exuded by rotting substances. And for centuries many people were just as certain that poisonous mushrooms grew from the nests of

21

vipers. The idea that mushrooms themselves might not be complete plants at all but only the fruits of plants, comparable to apples on a tree or grapes on a vine, was first proposed by biologists at the end of the 16th century.

The fungi are, in fact, as different from green plants, bacteria, and algae, as they are from animals. They reproduce and disseminate using spores, not seeds as do plants. In addition, while animals and plants reproduce through sexual union, most fungi multiply through somatic vegetative, or asexual, reproduction. But more importantly, fungi lack chlorophyll, the pigment essential for photosynthesis. Because of this they have to obtain their nutrients from other sources. Fungi that feed off dead or decaying plant or animal matter are called saprophytes; those that obtain their food supply

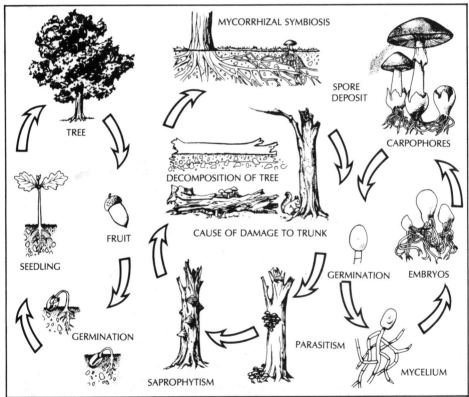

The life cycle of a fungus (right) is similar to that of a tree (left). Fungi can establish three types of relationships with plants: mycorrhizal symbiotic, parasitic, or saprophytic.

from living organisms are called parasites. These two categories, however, are not always rigid. There are fungi that will first live parasitically on a host, and, when the host dies, feed on the remains. These parasitic/saprophytic fungi are especially serious threats to crop plants. *to place or settle comfortably, snugly, or securely*

Today fungi are securely ensconced in their own separate kingdom, and mycology, the study of these organisms, is an important branch of the natural sciences. Fungal reproduction alone is a field that could occupy biologists for many years. Though there are many opinions regarding the number of fungal species in the world, scientists agree that in addition to the approximately 50,000 kinds of fungi that have been recognized and named, there is an equal number still waiting to be studied.

This puffball mushroom, which can grow to over a foot in diameter, is one of the types of fungi that disseminate their spores by exploding and shooting them into the air. Ultimately the fungi must rely on the wind to carry a few of its spores to a suitable environment.

Found some of this in greenhouse area on COS campus!

For most living and extinct plants and animals there is a fossil record that allows scientists to trace them back to their earliest forms. Primitive fungus-like structures have been discovered that may be among the oldest records of living things on earth. It is certain that by the Devonian Period, about 400 million years ago, there were many types of fungi growing amidst the green plants. However, it is impossible to determine which kind of living organism arose first. For fungi there is neither a definite starting point nor the connecting links that would allow a mycologist to construct the sort of evolutionary tree that exists for both the plant and animal kingdoms.

Scientists have not identified all of the many substances responsible for the effects of the psychedelic mushrooms. The fungi that have become known through their use in the religions, healing techniques, and mythologies of human populations represent only a few of the subjects of a field of scientific inquiry conceived as recently as in the 1950s. Certainly the search for increased knowledge will reveal many surprises about the uses of hallucinogenic mushrooms in human cultures and the effects they have upon their users.

Higher and Lower Fungi

Fungi are divided into two categories—the lower and the higher. The lower fungi are found just about everywhere—on or in humans, animals, birds, leaves, potatoes, grains, bread, feces, insect pollen, wood, soil, lichens, sand, peat, bone, snake skin, algae, and each other; and also in air, water, and even snow and ice. The vast majority are microscopic, visible in large concentrations as blue molds or matted threads.

The lower fungi are the chief causes of disease in plants. For example, *Claviceps purpurea* attacks grasses, especially rye, and produces hallucinogenic compounds that are structurally similar to LSD. These fungi were responsible for periodic outbreaks of ergot poisoning—St. Anthony's fire—reported to have occurred between the 11th century and 19th century in different parts of Europe. *Phytophthera infestans*, a lower fungus known as the potato blight, was responsible for the devastating Irish famines of the mid-19th century.

24

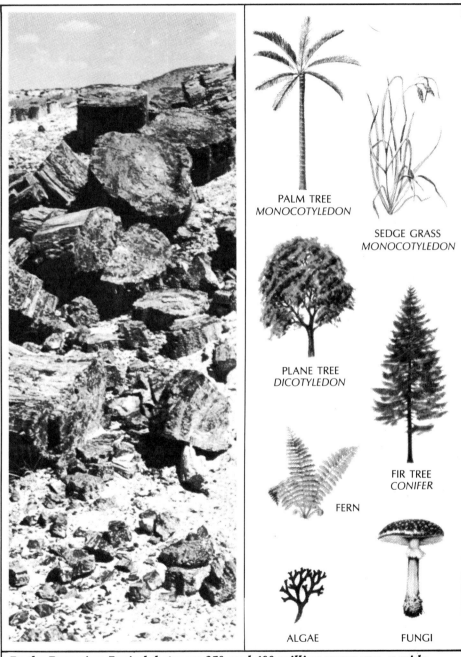

PALM TREE
MONOCOTYLEDON

SEDGE GRASS
MONOCOTYLEDON

PLANE TREE
DICOTYLEDON

FIR TREE
CONIFER

FERN

ALGAE

FUNGI

By the Devonian Period, between 350 and 400 million years ago, a wide variety of marine animals had evolved. Fossil evidence also shows that by this time many types of fungi were thriving amidst green plants.

Though the lower fungi cause potato blight, ringworm, athlete's foot, jungle rot, and other damage to humans, animals, food crops, and even manufactured goods, they also play a beneficial role in many industrial activities such as food processing, antibiotics manufacturing, fermentation, and vitamin synthesis. The green mold penicillium produces penicillin, the powerful antibiotic. And yeast, a type of single-celled fungi, contains such high-quality vitamins and proteins that the use of just 1.5 ounces of this organism in a loaf of bread will provide as much additional food value as two and a half eggs.

And finally, whether a fungal parasite is a bane or a boon may be in the eye—or on the taste buds—of the beholder. Corn smut is dreaded by European and American farmers, but was highly esteemed as a delicacy by the ancient Aztecs of pre-Columbian Mexico, and still is by many modern Mexicans.

The Mushrooms

Many animals, including primates, feed on mushrooms, and it is likely that wild fungi were an integral part of the diet of the most primitive of our hominid ancestors. While Ameri-

A medieval artist's fanciful vision of St. Anthony, patron saint of ergotism victims. In the Middle Ages the fungus ergot was sometimes inadvertently baked into bread. Those who ate it experienced what was called "St. Anthony's fire," whose symptoms included intense itching, gangrene, nervous spasms, hallucinations, and respiratory failure. Thousands died.

cans generally ingest only one or two species of cultivated mushrooms, in central and eastern Europe more than a dozen wild species are eaten. One Mexican Indian population distinguishes 57 different species of edible wild mushrooms, plus a few hallucinogenic types.

Of the five classes into which some authorities divide the fungal kingdom, the principal hallucinogenic species belong to the class Basidiomycetes. This class includes the mushrooms with the familiar umbrella shape (including *Amanita muscaria*, the brightly colored and inebriating fly agaric of Eurasia; the *Psilocybes*; and other psychoactive genera), as well as stinkhorns, earthstars, and puffballs. The puffballs include two species that produce pronounced auditory hallucinations.

Human beings have long appreciated the wild mushroom's value as food for body and soul, even though the fungi's sole function is to produce and disperse spores. Of the millions of spores that fall from even the smallest mushroom, very few actually reach a suitable spot for germination, which is possible only where temperature and moisture levels are ideal. Such a lucky spore will swell until it divides into two cells, each of which continues to absorb nutrients until it divides again. Eventually the multiplying

A 1943 photograph of penicillin. The drug, secreted by a Penicillium *mold, was the first of the "miracle" antibiotics that revolutionized the treatment of bacterial disease and saved countless lives.*

cells appear as very fine, cotton-like threads, called *hyphae*. Dense tangles of these threads form the *mycelium*, a subsurface fungal colony, the actual structure from which mushrooms sprout and surface (with the exception of such subterranean species as the truffle). And thus the cycle can begin again.

Mycorrhiza: Fungi and Higher Plants

Fungi, including the mushrooms, may be parasitic. This means that they benefit from a host organism while the host suffers and even dies. But there is another kind of relationship between certain fungi and higher plants from which both partners derive important, even vital, benefits. These symbiotic, or mutually beneficial, relationships—specifically called *mycorrhiza* (literally "fungus roots")—exist between fungi and most flowering plants, including forest trees. Mycorrhiza are so essential that without them the plants' growth would be retarded, sometimes severely so. The fungi also require these relationships for their own survival.

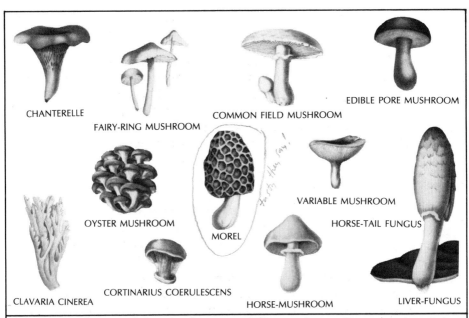

CHANTERELLE

FAIRY-RING MUSHROOM

COMMON FIELD MUSHROOM

EDIBLE PORE MUSHROOM

OYSTER MUSHROOM

MOREL

VARIABLE MUSHROOM

HORSE-TAIL FUNGUS

CLAVARIA CINEREA

CORTINARIUS COERULESCENS

HORSE-MUSHROOM

LIVER-FUNGUS

Edible mushrooms (above) take many different shapes. Because at certain stages in their growth many poisonous species closely resemble the edible varieties, foraging for wild mushrooms can be very dangerous.

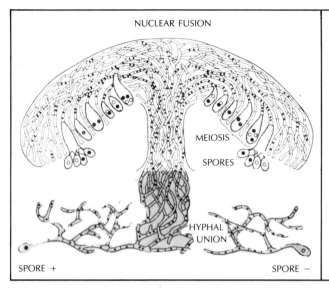

NUCLEAR FUSION

MEIOSIS

SPORES

HYPHAL UNION

SPORE +

SPORE −

Figure 2. *Schematic cross-section of a mushroom. Growth starts underground when the* hyphae, *cotton-like threads, develop from spore cells and unite to form the* mycelium, *a subsurface fungal colony. This, in turn, develops into the above-ground mushroom, which, when mature, produces new spores.*

The psychoactive fly agaric, *Amanita muscaria*, like other species of the genus *Amanita*, is one example of a mycorrhizal species. It is often symbiotically associated with birch ponderosa pine, lodgepole pine, aspen, cottonwood, spruce, Douglas fir, and some hardwoods, such as oak.

Mycorrhiza are more prevalent where there is plenty of light and a shortage of essential soil nutrients such as potassium, phosphorus, nitrogen, or calcium. The abundance of light causes the photosynthesizing plants to produce an excess of carbohydrates, which, in the form of sugars, provide the carbon required by mycorrhizal fungi. Able to use the complex compounds in the soil, the fungi in turn supply the host plant with essential nutrients. This exchange occurs through the fungal mycelia.

During fungal growth the mycelium spreads and the hyphae come into contact with very fine tree rootlets. There the hyphae attach themselves by forming a sheath-like covering of cells that enshroud the rootlet. This process is repeated hundreds of thousands of times as the mycelia gradually combine more and more with the tree's root system. Without this entanglement of rootlets and mycelia the symbiotic relationships would not be possible and the world's forests would not exist in the form that we know them.

As far back as 2,500 years ago Sanskrit poets celebrated the hallucinogenic drug Soma, now identified as fly agaric. In this illustration the gods and demons use the great snake, Vasuki, to churn the ocean of milk to obtain the sacred Soma.

CHAPTER 2

"MUSHROOMS OF THE GODS"

Why some fungi, like some plants, have evolved to contain toxins that, at the very least, can cause slight gastro-intestinal discomfort and at the worst, bring death, and why some others produce alkaloids with hallucinogenic effects, are questions with no simple answers. One can only con-clude that these species had an evolutionary advantage over more innocuous, nonhallucinatory species. Perhaps their bit-ter and acrid taste protected them against predation by browsing animals—at least until humans began to use the toxins to their advantage.

This hypothesis, however, does not explain the exis-tence of the fly agaric or the deadly "destroying angel," *Amanita Virosa*. When first ingested, the destroying angel is reputed to taste like a real delicacy. But as the pleasant taste lingers, the mushroom's poisons course through the body. By the time the adverse effects are noticed it is often too late.

The psychoactive mushrooms can be divided into two classes: those containing ibotenic acid and muscimol, and those containing psilocybin and its related alkaloids. The first class includes the fly agaric *A. muscaria*, and its close relative, *A. pantherina*. Only those mushrooms of the first class are known to have served as sacred inebriants in tribal cultures scattered across much of northern Siberia, in northern Scandinavia, and Finland, where the use of mushrooms are well-documented. There is reason to believe that the fly agaric was an integral part of ecstatic rituals in religions of pre-Christian Europe.

The ethnomycologist (a person who studies the cultural uses of mushrooms) R. Gordon Wasson has persuasively argued that Soma, the mysterious plant deity celebrated by the ancient Hindus in the *Rig Veda* (the great Sanskrit epic of the 2nd millenium B.C.E.), was this psychoactive mushroom. Its religious use is believed to have been primarily limited to the Old World, though sporadic occurrences of use in some native North American settings do hint at a wider cultural distribution in a former time.

Indra, Hindu god of the sky and storms (left), obtained his strength by drinking Soma, personified as a Hindu deity in an ancient wood carving (right). Supposedly, the gods gained immortality by ingesting Soma.

The only other area in the world where sacred or ritual use of psychoactive mushrooms has been documented is Mexico, though circumstantial evidence for their use in Guatemala and northern South America has also been found. However, the mushrooms used in this part of the world belong to several genera and numerous species chemically unrelated to the fly agaric and the other Eurasian mushrooms containing ibotenic acid and muscimol. These fungi, most of which belong to the genus *Psilocybe*, have as their active ingredient psilocybin and/or psilocin. All of the psychoactive members of this genus belong to the Caerulescentes (from the Latin caeruleus, meaning dark blue), so named because the stem beneath the cap stains caerulean blue

Mexican clay sculptures. A "mushroom man" from 100 B.C.E. (left). Cihateteo, the god of women who died in childbirth, with belt of mushrooms from 400 C.E. (center). Mushroom spirit from 1st century C.E..

when the fresh mushroom is scratched. The millenia-old phenomenon of sacred-mushroom use by Mexican Indians and the identification of the mushroom's extraordinary chemistry will be discussed later.

The genus *Psilocybe* has worldwide distribution, with 81 psychoactive species and 53 innocuous species. Thus far they have been identified in Southeast Asia, Melanesia, Japan, North Africa, Europe, and North, Central, and South America. However, in the New World the hallucinogenic *Psilocybe* species played a role in religious and psychotherapeutic ritual only among peoples south of the United States.

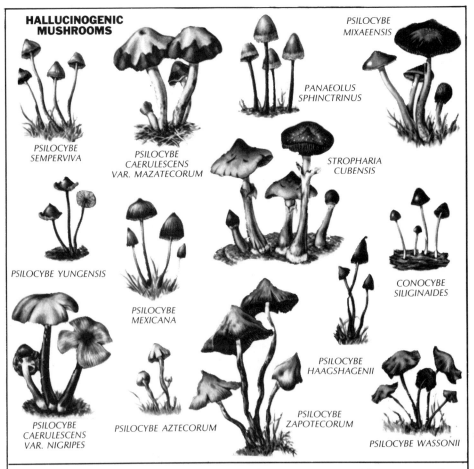

HALLUCINOGENIC MUSHROOMS

PSILOCYBE MIXAEENSIS

PANAEOLUS SPHINCTRINUS

PSILOCYBE SEMPERVIVA

PSILOCYBE CAERULESCENS VAR. MAZATECORUM

STROPHARIA CUBENSIS

PSILOCYBE YUNGENSIS

CONOCYBE SILIGINAIDES

PSILOCYBE MEXICANA

PSILOCYBE HAAGSHAGENII

PSILOCYBE CAERULESCENS VAR. NIGRIPES

PSILOCYBE AZTECORUM

PSILOCYBE ZAPOTECORUM

PSILOCYBE WASSONII

Psychoactive mushrooms take many different shapes and forms. Not all members of the genus **Psilocybe** *have hallucinogenic properties.*

Mushrooms have been very significant in the history of religion and psychotherapy. The same fly agaric to which the Sanskrit poets sang their praises in the Soma hymns of the *Rig Veda* in 1500 B.C.E. was the focus of a Bronze Age sun cult in Scandinavia. Indians in pre-Columbian Mexico carved stone idols of mushrooms 2500 years ago. The *Codex Vienna*—one of the few pre-Columbian pictorial manuscripts to survive the ravages of the Spanish Conquest of Mexico—identifies the sacred mushrooms as female earth deities, and credits the gods themselves with establishing the ritual of their use. Spanish clerics, after converting the Indians to Christianity, tried yet failed to uproot the mushrooms from their converts' religious life. Well into the 20th century the Laplanders in northern Finland and the tribal peoples of Siberia—especially the shamans, who were specialists in sacred matters, creators of ecstasy, and repositories of ancient knowledge—continued to use these fungi to raise themselves into states of divine inspiration and inebriation. Today psychoactive fungi are still employed by Mexican Indian peoples in divinatory psychotherapy (therapy that focuses on mental and/or emotional problems).

In the United States the existence of hallucinogenic mushrooms did not long remain a secret to those people interested in recreational psychedelics. Where wild-growing, psilocybin-containing species are relatively abundant—particularly in the Gulf States and the Pacific Northwest—mushroom use is common. In the Pacific Northwest the fly agaric and its sister species, *Amanita pantherina*, are popular recreational hallucinogens. *Psilocybe* mushrooms are also frequently cultivated in homes or in laboratories.

A Siberian rock carving thought to depict a shaman, or tribal holy man and healer, crowned with a mushroom, possibly the fly agaric, Amanita muscaria.

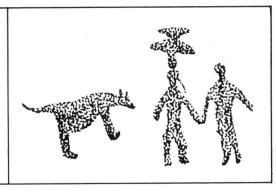

Even though for thousands of years many cultures have safely incorporated the use of psychoactive mushrooms into their customs and rituals, and despite a lack of evidence that the substances that they contain are dangerous or addictive, unauthorized possession, sale, and use of psilocybin or psilocin, or any substances containing these alkaloids—in other words, the mushrooms themselves—are illegal in the United States. The sacred mushrooms and other plant hallucinogens that the Indians had used for religious rites and divinatory healing have been declared against the law by the Mexican government. In part this was a reaction to the many young Americans and Europeans who, in the 1960s, traveled to native communities searching for the Truth they hoped to discover in the mushroom vision. But also, the Mexican

Many "flower children" of the 1960s, such as this woman who rented a shack from a Guatemalan Indian, flocked to Native American communities seeking psychedelic mushrooms and their effects.

action reflected the United States' war on drugs, which, while attempting to contain the epidemic use of truly dangerous drugs, included the use of psychedelic mushrooms among its targets though there is no evidence that pure mushrooms are at all dangerous. The inconsistencies in drug laws are further illustrated by the lack of restrictions placed on the use of tobacco and alcohol, two substances known to be addictive and hazardous to one's health.

However, an important question not often, or loudly enough, raised is, Why are Americans willing to risk so much—legally, economically, medically, and psychologically—for a brief alteration of their state of consciousness? Unfortunately, the issue of drug use all too often is reduced to statistical, legal, and medical insignificance.

The Potato Eaters, *an 1885 painting by Dutch artist Vincent Van Gogh. When fungus destroyed the potato crop in Ireland in the 1840s, thousands of people died of starvation or disease.*

The birch tree, which lives symbiotically with the fly agaric, was the Siberian shaman's sacred Tree of Life. Siberian tribal life included ritualistic as well as nonreligious uses of psychoactive mushrooms.

CHAPTER 3

AMANITA MUSCARIA: THE SACRED MUSHROOM OF SIBERIA

*S*ince the time of Tsar Peter the Great (1672–1725), the Kamchatka Peninsula, the easternmost part of Russian Siberia, has been visited by foreign travelers, explorers, political exiles, fur traders, prisoners of war, and, finally, anthropologists. It was here that they observed the nomadic reindeer herders and seashore hunters who, by ingesting psychoactive mushrooms, experienced out-of-body "flights" to otherworlds and had encounters with spirit beings. These native people consumed the flesh of a fungus many Europeans were convinced was fatally poisonous.

Few of the early observers were equipped to understand the significance of what they saw and heard. Nor did they realize that before Christianity came to Europe, sacred mushroom cults similar to those of the Siberian tribal peoples played a role in the religious lives of their own ancestors. In the 17th century many people determined the age of the earth from passages in the Bible, and therefore the idea that a mushroom cult might date back thousands of

39

years before the birth of Jesus seemed preposterous to anyone but a handful of natural historians.

It was a Japanese merchant named Denbei who first brought news of the magic mushrooms of Kamchatka back to Europe. When his ship was blown off course, Denbei, while seeking refuge in the estuary of a small Kamchatka river, was captured by tribesmen. Eventually he was freed by a Russian explorer who took him to Moscow and presented him at the tsar's court as the first Japanese on Russian soil. Among Denbei's descriptions of native life in Kamchatka was the use of fly agaric mushrooms. His story was remarkable not because the ritualistic use of mushrooms was unknown, but because it showed that this practice extended into the farthest reaches of the tsar's empire—all the way to the shores of the Bering Sea. Previously this phenomenon had been observed only in a Siberian region nearer to the Urals, the mountain range separating European and Asiatic Russia.

In 1658 Adam Kanienski Dluzyk, a Polish prisoner of war who for a short time lived with Ob-Ugrian tribesmen in

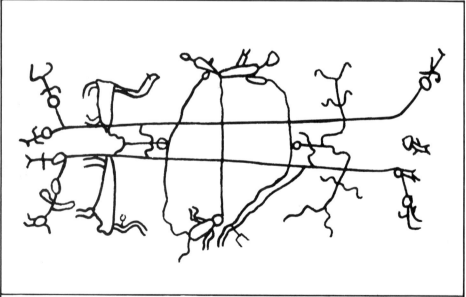

A Chukchi tribesman of eastern Siberia made this drawing of the wanderings of the fly-agaric men. The incorporation of deer on the left emphasizes the importance of this animal in these people's lives.

western Siberia, wrote that the natives knew nothing of agriculture, lived on the plentiful supply of game and fish, and wore clothing made from fish, geese, and/or swan skins. He also mentioned that the tribesmen became intoxicated on the highly esteemed fly agaric.

For the next two and a half centuries Westerners returned to their homelands with similar accounts from different parts of the giant Siberian wilderness—from the valleys of the Ob and Yenisei rivers in the west to the Bering Sea in the east. Though many reports conveyed the details of the nonreligious use of these mushrooms, there was little information regarding the role that mushrooms played in the religious life of the native peoples. As devout Christians these early travelers were either unable or unwilling to conceive of the beliefs and rituals of tribal folk as religion.

However, at the beginning of the 20th century, Russian anthropologists began an in-depth study of the traditional cultures of two of the Far Eastern, mushroom-using tribes—the Koryak of Kamchatka, and the Chukchi, their northern

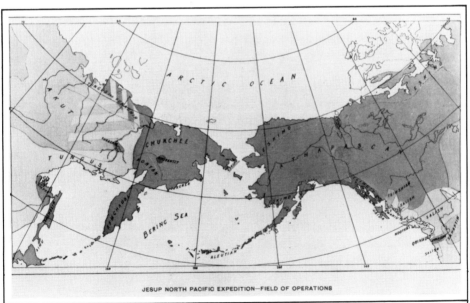

JESUP NORTH PACIFIC EXPEDITION—FIELD OF OPERATIONS

At the beginning of the 20th century the American Museum of Natural History organized expeditions to study mushroom cults among the natives of Siberia and Alaska (shaded area). There they found ritualistic use of the fly agaric.

neighbors living near the Arctic Circle. About half of each population was still living as nomadic reindeer herders and hunters in the interior, while the other half had become coastal fishermen and marine mammal hunters.

Russian colonization of this part of Siberia had begun in the mid-17th century, yet the native peoples had largely preserved their traditions and their religious beliefs and customs. Though the effects of the 1917 Russian Revolution would later reach even the most distant and isolated tribal cultures, during the first part of the 20th century anthropologists were able to enter a native universe that surely echoed—if it did not precisely mirror—the life styles and world views of people who lived centuries and even thousands of years before.

The Birth of the Mushroom Spirits

The Koryaks' story of the origin of the fly agaric is part of their sacred history, a compilation of tales handed down from generation to generation. The tales speak of an ancient mythological time when animals and people were one and the same, and when the culture hero, Big Raven—part trickster, part powerful shaman/magician—assisted the gods in putting the world in order.

Many cultures around the world have stories of Big Raven's magical exploits as a creator and transformer of natural phenomena, and of his deceitful pranks that often backfired on him. But only the creation myths of the Koryaks tell of the powerful little mushroom spirits, called *wa'paq*, that give people the feeling of superior strength and exhilaration and the power to see remote and unknown things. The story of the origin of the fly agaric was told to the Russian anthropologist Vladimir Bogoras:

> One day Big Raven found a whale that had strayed too far inland and had become beached on the shore. Big Raven tried to send his friend the whale back to his companions in the open sea, but found he could not even lift the grass bag in which Whale carried his provisions. Big Raven flew into the sky and appealed to the great deity Vahiyinen [existence] for advice. Vahiyinen told Big Raven to go to a certain level place near the sea, where

he would find white, stalk-like spirit beings wearing spotted, crimson-colored hats—the *wa'paq* spirits. If he ate some of them he would gain the strength to lift the bag and assist Whale in returning to deep water.

Big Raven went to the place where he was to meet the *wa'paq*, and there Vahiyinen spat upon the earth. Wherever his spittle fell, fly-agaric mushrooms sprang up. It was they who were the *wa'paq*. After Big Raven ate some of the *wa'paq* he felt so strong and gay that he started to dance.

The fly-agaric spirits asked him how it was that he, being such a great and powerful man, could not even lift Whale's provision bag. Big Raven replied, "You are quite right. I am a strong man, so I shall go and lift the traveling bag."

He returned to where the whale was beached, picked up the heavy grass bag as though it weighed nothing, and sent Whale on his way. Then Big Raven said, "Let the fly agaric remain on earth forever, and let my children, the people, see what it will show them."

A carved raven from the northwest coast of North America. One Koryak myth relates how Big Raven, a trickster and shaman, met the wa'paq, *the mushroom spirits, and introduced them to the world.*

From then on, Koryak shamans did as Big Raven had done—eating fly-agaric mushrooms to gain knowledge and supernatural strength, to conjure animal and spirit beings, and to project their souls into otherworlds. The word "shaman" is a term derived from the Siberian Tungus *saman*, meaning diviner, magician, doctor, creators of ecstasy, specialist in the sacred, and mediator between the human world and the supernatural.

The Koryaks and other Siberian peoples believed that anyone—even if he or she were not a shaman—who ate *wa'paq* would be told the future, the nature and origin of an illness, and the meaning of dreams. In addition, by ingesting the *wa'paq* a person in the mushroom-induced, ecstatic trance would be able to travel to the realm of celestial beings and return with news of dead relatives.

A Koryak shaman—the mediator between humans and the supernatural—in the Kamchatka region of eastern Siberia. Following the sacred example of Big Raven, Koryak shamans believed that the fly agaric could tell them about illness, the future, and the meaning of dreams.

The Fly Agaric: Truth and Fiction

The *wa'paq* spirits of the Koryak are the same white-spotted, crimson toadstools that for centuries have been associated with European fairytales and magic. Because of this association these mushrooms gained the reputation of being fatally poisonous and thus elicited fear in anyone who came across them. The origin of the generic title, *Amanita*, is uncertain, but some authorities believe it to be derived from Mount Amanon in Cilicia, a Roman province in the southern area of modern Turkey. The fly agaric's species name, *muscaria*, comes from the Latin *musca*, meaning fly.

Though the word "toadstool" now stands for any poisonous or inedible wild mushroom, formerly it referred specifically to the fly agaric. Many Celtic, Scandinavian, and other European languages have words that link this mushroom with the toad. Toads long ago gained the undeserved reputation for causing warts and throughout history they have been associated with witches and the Devil. But in pre-Christian Europe, as in pre-Colombian Mexico and South America, the toad was linked with female fertility and the life-giving Mother Goddess. Perhaps it is because of this latter sacred role that people connected the spirit of the earth—the toad—and the fly agaric.

A three-inch-tall figure of a shaman under what appears to be Amanita muscaria, *or fly agaric. This pre-Columbian ceramic, found in Nayarit, Mexico, is almost 2000 years old.*

Central Europeans no longer use the inebriating mushroom in pagan religious rites, as they presumably did before the advent of Christianity, but something of its former supernatural aura lingers on. For example, to a riddle that asks, "What little man stands in the forest, perched on one leg and wrapped in a brilliant red cape?" German children shout with delight, *"Der Gluckspilz, der Gluckspilz!"* (mushroom of good luck, good fortune). And fly agarics are still considered proper decorations for Christmas trees in Germany.

There are many European folktales that give accounts of the fly agaric-mushroom's magical origin that are reminiscent of the one in the Koryak tale. For example, one tale tells of Jesus and Peter, who had been traveling for a long time without food. However, unbeknownst to Jesus, Peter had a loaf of bread concealed in his knapsack. When the two were passing through a forest, he secretly slipped a piece of bread into his mouth. At that very moment Jesus asked a question and in order to answer Peter had to spit the piece out. This happened several times, until all the loaf was gone.

Mushrooms and toadstools are a part of the mythology and folklore of many cultures, whether discovered by Alice in Wonderland (left) or associated with elves. This may be due to the fungi's surprisingly rapid growth in woods as well as to their psychoactive properties.

But wherever the bread touched the ground, edible mushrooms sprang up. The Devil, who was following them at a distance, saw this and decided he could produce brighter and more brilliantly colored mushrooms. However, when he spat out pieces of bread onto the forest floor, marvelously colored but inedible and poisonous mushrooms appeared.

Yugoslav peasants remember another version that takes the supernatural origin of fly-agaric mushrooms back into the time of the pre-Christian nature gods. One day, so goes the legend, Votan, chief of all the gods and a potent magician and healer, was riding his magical steed through the countryside. Suddenly demons appeared and started chasing him. Votan's horse galloped faster and faster, until blood-flecked foam flew in all directions from his mouth. Wherever the bloody foam fell, red and white fly-agaric mushrooms sprang up!

The Europeans have not quite forgotten the mushroom's peculiar effects. Austrians and Germans speak of "fool's mushrooms" and "mad mushrooms." In Vienna, instead of asking, "Have you gone out of your mind?" or "Have you lost your senses?" people are apt to ask if you have eaten *verruckte*

Votan, or Odin, the chief god in Norse mythology, on his throne in Valhalla overlooking heaven and earth. The two ravens, representing thought and memory— the paired halves of consciousness—were said to fly back to Votan each day to whisper the secrets of the universe. The ravens' roles are very similar to the function of fly agaric in the Siberian mushroom-using tribes.

Schwammerl, "crazy mushrooms." The Hungarians call the fly agaric *boland gomba,* or the "mad mushroom."

The German word *fliegenpilz,* "fly mushroom," comes from the mushroom's reputation and popular use as a natural insecticide. Flies that land on its blood-red cap or feed on milk in which a mushroom has been soaked were, and in some places still are, believed to fall into a stupor and die. Some Europeans still place fly agarics or the milk-mushroom preparation on their window sills to kill flies. In fact, scien-

A nomadic Lapp youngster with his pet reindeer in northern Finland. Laplanders continued to use hallucinogenic mushrooms to reach states of divine inspiration well into the 20th century.

tific experiments have shown that these mushrooms can be lethal to flies.

In their book *Russia, Mushrooms & History*, R. G. and Valentina P. Wasson have suggested an additional, or alternate, explanation for the popular name. They recalled that for hundreds or even thousands of years, insects, particularly flies, have been associated with divine possession, intoxication, and madness (hence, the Russians use the expression *on c mukhoj*, being "with fly," when a person has had too much to drink). And in pre-Christian mythology gods and demons often appeared in the guise of flies and other flying insects. As the old gods were transformed into Satan and his companions, flies too became creatures of the Devil. In fact, Satan got his epithet "Lord of Flies" from Ba'al or Beelzebub, an Old Testament god worshiped by neighbors of the Israelites and whose Hebrew name, Ba'al Zevuv, means lord of the fly.

Finally, over the years, the facts and legends about the fly agaric converged, mixing the truths about the fly's fatal attraction to the mushroom with the tales about the pagan gods and divine possession. Even today, for many people around the world the mention of the fly agaric reverberates with the richness and strength of its history.

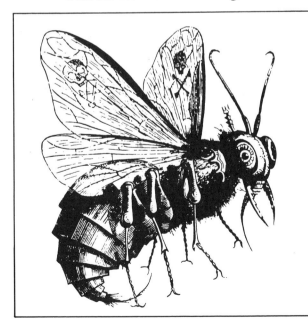

Beelzebub, Lord of the Flies, as illustrated in the Dictionnaire Infernal, *was an epithet for Satan that was taken from pre-Christian mythology. Flies have been associated with divine possession and intoxication for thousands of years.*

A mature fly agaric of a variety found in the northeastern United States. The split in the edge of the cap is an indication that the mushroom is preparing to release millions of microscopic spores.

CHAPTER 4

MORPHOLOGY AND ECOLOGY OF THE FLY AGARIC

Visually, the toadstool is one of the most beautiful members of the fungal kingdom. Often as tall as 8 or 9 inches, the Eurasian and the western North American varieties are readily identified by their bright blood-red caps dotted with white "warts," and their thick, cylindrical, hollow stems, which are white with several concentric ringlets of scales just above the swelling bulb at the base. The gills, or radiating plates, on the underside of the cap range from white to cream.

There are several varieties of *A. muscaria*, differentiated from one another primarily by the pigments of the cap, veil, stem, and bottom bulb or cup. Mycologists recognize five varieties of *A. muscaria* and four of the closely related *A. pantherina*. The most common *A. muscaria* variety in Europe and western North America is blood-red, whereas the caps of the varieties native to the northern and eastern United States range in color from orange-red to yellow and even to white. Only a few of these varieties have been examined for their degree of toxicity.

Varieties of *A. pantherina* are found in mixed forests in the Pacific Northwest of the United States and Canada, in the northeastern, midwestern, and southeastern United States, and in eastern Canada. Their caps range in color from light to rich brown and they are covered with irregularly distributed, soft, white warts. There is as much misinformation regarding this species as there is about the fly agaric. Mush-

A shaman of the Mapuche region of Chile communicating with the spirits at the top level of the World Tree. Hallucinogenic plants may have helped in her ascent.

room manuals generally describe it as being deadly poisonous, though it is no more poisonous than A. muscaria. A. pantherina contains the same intoxicating chemicals as A. muscaria, though in considerably higher amounts.

Like other species of the genus Amanita, A. muscaria is a mycorrhizal mushroom, closely associated with certain trees and other plants. In North America, as in Europe and Asia, the fly agaric's preferred habitat is birch forests or stands of birch in mixed forests. They are most numerous in late summer and fall.

The fly agaric's symbiotic relationship is by no means limited only to birches and their close relatives; however, it is probably not a coincidence that in Siberia the birch was preeminently the sacred tree of shamans. It was their Tree of Life and the "ladder" on which the shaman symbolically ascended to the heavens. Shamans enacted that celestial journey by climbing into the crowns of the trees, where they perched, pounding their drums and chanting sacred songs while in a state of ecstasy. There is no reason to believe that all, or even most, Siberian shamans resorted to ingesting A. muscaria or any intoxicants. On the contrary, drumming, chanting, and other non-drug-related techniques for attaining an ecstatic state were probably more widely employed than chewing on the fly agaric.

In mushroom guides and in some dictionaries, the fly agaric is sometimes grouped with two other Amanitas: A. phalloides, the "death cap," and A. virosa, the "destroying angel." The three are described as being the species most responsible for fatal or near-fatal cases of mushroom poisoning. While this lethalness is certainly true for the death cap and destroying angel, it is not true for the fly agaric.

Though the toxins of the fly agaric are psychoactive, or hallucinogenic, and not deadly, still, ingestion of this fungus is not without its unpleasant side effects. Moreover, one race of the species may have different proportions of toxins than one in another region. Because of the many variables, it is dangerous for people inexperienced in mushrooms to consume this or any wild mushroom. Even the Koryak and their neighbors—whose use of mushrooms was incorporated into their rituals—understood that for some individuals the consumption of the fly agaric might be followed by severe sickness and, in exceptional cases, even death.

The Fly Agaric's Deadly Cousins

One way to differentiate the edible and poisonous mushroom species from *A. muscaria* is by color. The cap of the
deadly *A. phalloides* ranges from light yellow to greenish
brown, and that of the equally deadly *A. virosa* is pure
white, occasionally with a rosy shade at the apex. However,
proper identification is not this simple and straightforward.
There are North American species of *Amanita* that have not
been adequately studied and thus may or may not be poisonous. Also, occasionally fly agarics exhibit a very light
yellow to white cap somewhat similar to those of its poisonous cousins.

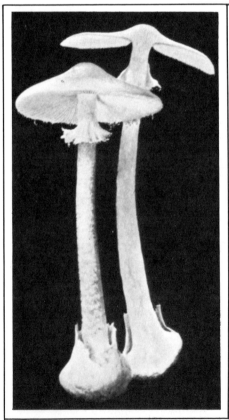 

Two types of Amanita: A. pantherina, *or the panther (left), and* A. virosa, *or
the destroying angel. Though* A. virosa *is lethal,* A. pantherina *is no more
toxic than the fly agaric.*

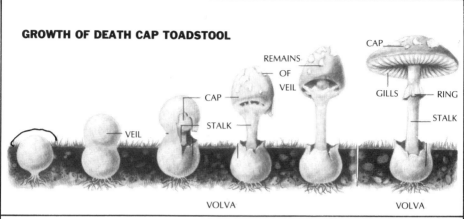

GROWTH OF DEATH CAP TOADSTOOL

Figure 3. *Stages in the growth of* A. phalloides, *or the death cap, ingestion of which is usually fatal. After emerging from the ground enclosed in a veil, the stalk elongates and forces the veil to split, after which the cap separates from the stalk, leaving a prominent ring.*

Though folk wisdom claims that edible and deadly mushroom species can be differentiated by determining if a particular species turns a silver spoon black, in fact, both edible and deadly species may or may not do this. A more reliable test is to examine the stem. One of the principal characteristics of the death cup and its cousins, destroying angel and *A. verna*, "spring amanita," is that they appear to be growing out of a well-defined, jagged-edged cup. This pronounced cup is lacking in *A. muscaria* and also in various harmless *Amanitas*.

This cup, or *volva*, is the remains of the *universal veil*, the thick membrane that envelops the fruit body of some mushrooms, including the *Amanitas*, in their early stages. When the Ping-Pong-ball-shaped immature mushroom bursts from the ground, it quickly elongates and the universal veil breaks away, exposing the stem, cap, and gills. In the deadly *Amanitas* the remains of the veil form the distinctive volva. Fragments of this same veil also adhere to the top of the cap, visible as the familiar white warts, especially striking in the crimson variety of the fly agaric. In the *Amanitas*, the fragile gills, which protect the spores, are initially enclosed by another membrane, the partial veil, which also bursts as the cap begins to flatten out, leaving veil-like remnants on the stalk.

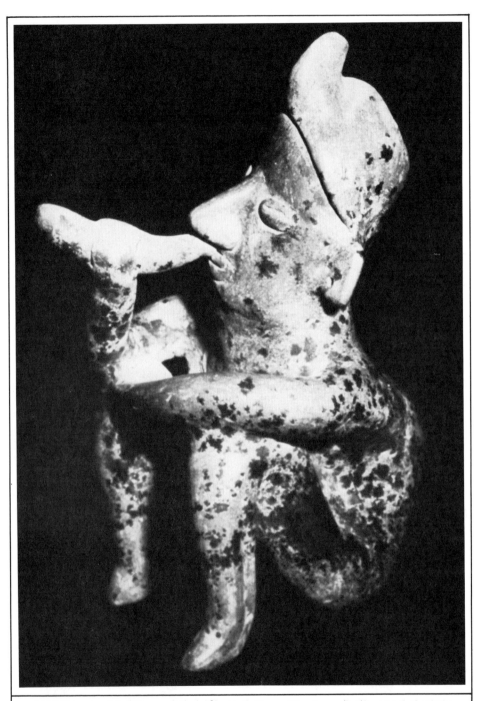

A 2000-year-old clay sculpture from Colima, Mexico, of a horned shaman with a pipe for ingesting psychoactive snuff. Similar use of snuff in pre-Columbian South and Central America is well documented.

CHAPTER 5

EFFECTS OF PHALLOTOXINS

After ingestion, the phallotoxins—poisons of the deadly mushrooms—are slow to take effect. Symptoms of mushroom poisoning rapidly progress from light to severe gastrointestinal distress to diarrhea and finally to convulsive vomiting. If appropriate countermeasures are not undertaken at once, death may result.

Unfortunately, even if medical help is available, damage to the body quickly results. Once *phalloidin* and *amanitin*, the two principal phallotoxins in *A. phalloides*, have entered the bloodstream they rapidly destroy the tissues of the liver and kidneys. Because this mushroom is so delicious when cooked, cases of poisoning have usually been the result of deliberate harvesting and ingestion by adult mushroom hunters who thought it was an edible species.

Three Stages of Intoxication

Both the Koryaks and the Chukchis usually dried the mushrooms and strung them together in threes—the average dose. When dry the mushrooms were shredded into small pieces, and chewed with a little water, one morsel at a time. Among the Koryak it was customary for the wife to chew the mushroom and then offer the moistened quid to her husband. Chukchi men, however, generally chewed the fly agaric for themselves. Members of the Siberian Kamchadal tribe rolled the dried fungus into a tube and either swallowed it unchewed or soaked it in a willow-herb concoction and then drank this tincture.

The intoxicating effects came on suddenly, usually within a quarter of an hour after ingestion. Most often the person remained awake, although it was considered better to fall asleep immediately after eating the mushrooms, and awaken only when thoroughly under the influence of the fly agaric.

There were generally three stages to mushroom intoxication, though these stages frequently intermingled, especially among older, experienced users. Initially, the mushroom eater felt pleasantly excited, and often felt an increase in his or her agility and strength. Reindeer hunters on the Middle Anadyr River said that if they chewed fly agaric before launching their canoes they became more nimble

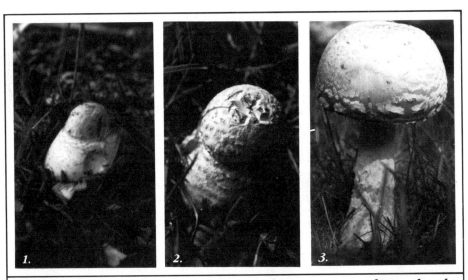

The three-day life cycle of the fly agaric. 1. The immature mushroom breaks through the ground. 2. The rounded cap as it begins to differentiate from the stem. 3. The universal veil has broken.

on the hunt. In fact, one Chukchi who accompanied the distinguished Russian anthropologist Vladimir Bogoras on one of his overland trips would chew fly agaric and then lay aside his snowshoes and walk for hours with his dogs through the deep snow. He claimed it was "for the mere pleasure of exercise, and without any feeling of fatigue."

Earlier travelers in Siberia also referred to a remarkable increase in physical prowess as a result of eating the mushroom. Adolf Erman, who visited Kamchatka during his world travels between 1828 and 1831, wrote that there was "no doubt about a marvelous increase in physical strength," which tribesmen claimed as one of the effects of fly-agaric intoxication. "In harvesting hay," one man told him, "if I have eaten a mushroom I can do the work of three men from morning to nightfall without any trouble." Thus, it seems that the fly agaric turns the myth of Big Raven and Whale into reality.

During this first stage of intoxication the traditional mushroom eater would often sing and dance, frequently breaking into loud peals of laughter. This behavior is reminiscent of Big Raven's initial reaction to *wa'paq*.

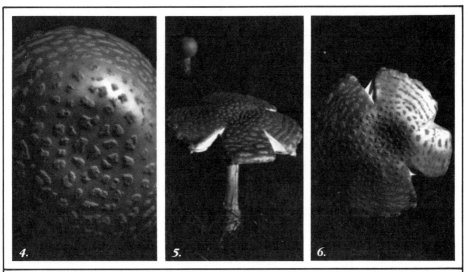

4. Close-up of white warts, the remnants of the veil, on the red cap.
5. Flattened and split cap after spores have been released. 6. Close-up of flattened and split cap.

During the second stage of intoxication a person experienced hallucinations. He might hear strange voices bidding him to perform bizarre acts. Though the surrounding world was still recognizable, spirits might appear and even converse with the mushroom eater. Objects appeared to be enlarged—a knife handle might seem so huge that it had to be grasped with both hands; or a doorsill might look so large that, upon entering a room, the user would lift his or her feet exceedingly high.

Sometimes the mushroom eaters would feel themselves transformed into a spirit, which the Chukchi say look exactly like the mushrooms themselves. One man put a bag over his head and violently pulled at it, trying to burst through the bottom "as though he were a young mushroom bursting

A tapestry of a man and woman beneath a psychoactive mushroom woven by the late Huichol Indian artist and shaman Ramon Médina.

forth from the ground." Another man lowered his head until it seemed he had no neck, bent his knees to shorten his legs, and scurried about, explaining that the fly-agaric spirits, always moving about with great speed, have no necks or legs but only stout, cylindrical bodies and wide hats.

The effects of the third stage of intoxication are much more extreme. Though no longer conscious of his or her surroundings, the mushroom user continued to be active— walking about, sometimes raving incoherently, occasionally even breaking things.

Like other Asiatic and American Indian peoples, the Chukchi felt the world was multi-layered—several layers of heaven above and several layers of underworld below the earth's surface, all connected by a cosmic central axis. Each cosmic level, in turn, had its ruling spirits. In times of communal or individual crisis, the shamans traveled to these different levels to consult with the spirits. Normally only shamans could do this, but with the help of the mushroom spirits, even ordinary people could make such journeys. It remained for the shaman, however, to interpret the user's

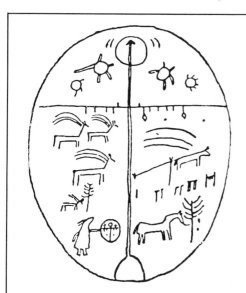 

Ceremonial drums are an integral part of many rituals. A drawing from an Icelandic shaman's drum (left) shows the world tree, roots in the underworld, trunk in the inhabited earth, and crown in the realm of the gods. At right is an abstract drawing of a shaman found on a Lapp drum.

experience to his or her fellow tribesmen. The trance journey was followed by a heavy sleep so deep that it was often impossible to rouse the sleeper. This might last for up to several hours.

Light fly-agaric intoxication was often accompanied by varying degrees of animation and spontaneous movements, alternated with moments of deep depression. Stronger intoxication produced hallucinations. Intoxicated persons sometimes sat quietly, rocking from side to side, even taking part in conversations with the family. But suddenly the eyes would dilate, and wild gesticulations and conversations with invisible persons would begin. This was often followed by a period of rest. However, additional doses were frequently ingested to maintain the same level of intoxication. Finally there occurred a deep slumber followed by a headache, sensations of nausea, and an urge to repeat the intoxication.

Some experienced mushroom users could eat up to 10 fungi without experiencing hazardous effects, though some individuals become intoxicated after ingesting as few as three. There was a report of one Koryak who swallowed 10 mushrooms without feeling any effects. But after he swallowed one more he began to vomit, and soon died. The Koryak attributed the death to strangulation by the spirits of the fly agaric, which manifested themselves in the form of worms.

The Koryak believed that a person intoxicated by the mushrooms did what the *wa'paq* spirits residing in them told him or her to do. "Here I am, lying here and feeling so sad," one elder said, "but, should I eat some agaric, I should get up and commence to talk and dance. There is an old man with white hair. If he should eat some agaric, and if he were told by it, 'You have just been born,' the old man would at once begin to cry like a new-born baby. Or, if the agaric should say to a man, 'You will melt away soon,' then the man would see his legs, arms, and body melt away, and he would say, 'Oh, why have I eaten of the agaric? Now I am gone.' Or, should the agaric say, 'Go to The-One-On-High,' the man would go to The-One-On-High. The latter would put him in the palm of his hand and twist him like a thread, so that his bones would crack, and the entire world would twirl around. 'Oh, I am dead!' that man would say, 'Why have I eaten the agaric?' But when he came to, he would eat it again, because sometimes it is pleasant and cheerful. Besides, the agaric would tell every man, even if he were not a shaman, what ailed him when he was sick, or explain a dream to him, or show him the upper world or the underground world, or foretell what would happen to him."

Death, *a 16th-century sculpture by French artist Ligier Richier. Koryak tribesmen believe that if the fly agaric tells a man he will melt away, he will soon see his legs, arms, and body begin to disappear.*

"A Vision of Hell"

The subjective mushroom experience of Europeans greatly differed from that of native peoples. In a description of Kamchatka published in 1755, the explorer Stepan Krasheninnikov tells of a Cossack who, after ingesting mushrooms, "had a vision of Hell as a terrifying, fiery chasm into which he was to be cast." The *mukhomor* (the Russian word for fly agaric) ordered him to go down on his knees and "confess all the sins that he could remember committing," which he did in front of his friends, thinking that he was doing so "in the privacy of the sacrament to God

The subjective effects of intoxicating mushrooms are shaped by the user's background. One Russian, after ingesting mushrooms, had a vision of hell similar to that pictured in this medieval drawing.

alone." The mushroom spirit had readily adapted to the European's religious background and continued to speak with authority.

Joseph Kopec, a Polish brigadier, had a much more positive mushroom experience when, after falling seriously ill while in Kamchatka in 1797 or 1798, he called for his confessor. The priest, who had some knowledge of medicine, prescribed fly agaric "as the most precious creation of nature" to help him sleep. The Polish officer reluctantly swallowed part of the mushroom and fell into a deep sleep filled with visions of "the most attractive gardens where only pleasure and beauty seemed to rule," and where beautiful white-clad women offered him fruits, berries, and flowers. He so hated to leave these visions that he was distressed to find himself awake again. Toward evening he asked for a second helping. This time he ingested an entire mushroom and fell into a deep sleep in which "new visions carried me to another world," where after a time he was ordered to return to earth so that a priest could take his confession. He awoke, asked for a priest, confessed, and again fell into a profound sleep from which he did not awaken for 24 hours.

An Early Scientific Inquiry

Georg Heinrich von Langsdorf, an early German explorer of Kamchatka, was far more interested in the natural history and chemistry of the fly agaric, and in the experiences of tribal peoples, than in the Europeans' often frivolous or even medicinal use of the mushrooms. In 1809 he published a scientific paper entirely devoted to the use and effects of the fly agaric, and in which he named the Kamchatkan species *Amanita muscaria*, of the variety *Camschatica*.

The mushrooms, he reported, grew in birch forests and on dry plains and almost everywhere else in Kamchatka, but they were most abundant in the central part of the peninsula. The Kamchadal usually harvested them in July and August, the hottest months, and let them dry in the earth. They believed that preparing them in this fashion produced more potent mushrooms than those picked fresh or strung up to dry. Smaller specimens with bright red caps covered with many white warts were said to be more potent than larger, paler red mushrooms with few white spots. Sometimes the mushrooms were cooked fresh and eaten in soups or sauces; in this form they had a weaker effect and thus could be consumed in greater quantities. Occasionally, too, fly agarics were soaked in berry juice and the concoction was then drunk as though it were wine.

Von Langsdorf noted that the same person might experience considerably different effects on separate occasions. Sometimes a single mushroom would produce intense effects in an individual, while at other times as many as a dozen would have little effect at all.

The effects noted by von Langsdorf have been mentioned in modern accounts of mushroom users. Persons slightly intoxicated feel extraordinarily light on their feet and exceedingly agile and skillful. And, as previously mentioned, there is the tendency for objects to appear larger than they actually are. Von Langsdorf observed intoxicated persons jumping over small sticks as if they were tree trunks.

The mushroom's psychoactive ingredients also tend to amplify a person's normal behavior. For example, someone ordinarily gregarious will become even more talkative; one fond of dancing will dance incessantly; and a music lover will sing at the top of his lungs. In this "intense and stimulated state of the nervous system," the explorer reported, "these persons exert muscular efforts of which they would

German toxicologist Louis Lewin was the first scientist to study psychoactive plants. His 1924 book Phantastica *examined some 28 plants used around the world for their stimulating effects.*

be completely incapable at other times; for example, they have carried heavy burdens with the greatest of ease, and eyewitnesses have confirmed to me the fact that a person in a state of fly-agaric ecstasy carried a 120-pound sack of flour the distance of 10 miles."

Fly Agaric and Urine Drinking

One extraordinary aspect of Siberian fly-agaric inebriation, generally misunderstood and noted with shock by European observers, was the consumption of urine of mushroom users that was suffused with the fly-agaric alkaloids.

Anthropologist Bogoras wrote:

> *Drinking the urine of one who has recently eaten fly agaric produces the same effects as eating the mushroom. The passion for intoxication becomes so strong that when the mushrooms are scarce, people will often resort to this source when agaric is not available. Apparently without aversion they will even pass this liquor around in their ordinary tea cups.*

And about the Koryak, anthropologist Jochelson reported:

> *There is reason to think that the effects of fly-agaric would be stronger were not its alkaloids quickly removed from the organism with the urine. The Koryak know this by experience, and the urine of persons intoxicated with fly-agaric is not wasted. The drinker himself drinks it to prolong the state of hallucination, or offers it to others as a treat. According to the Koryak, the urine of one intoxicated by fly agaric has an intoxicating effect like the fungus, though not to so great a degree. In the village of Paren I saw a company of fly-agaric eaters using a can, in which California fruit had been put up, as a beaker into which the urine was passed, to be drunk afterward.*

Even as late as the turn of the century, when anthropologists began to briefly report the custom with proper scientific detachment, some western writers could not refrain from treating the phenomenon as just one more example of the "disgusting habits of the uncivilized, non-Christian Asiatic tribesmen." Only von Langsdorf's inquiry of the early 1800s was serious, dispassionate, and truly scientific.

Not content with mere description, he intelligently speculated about the specific nature of the hallucinogenic alkaloid which retained its strength even after passing through not just one body, but several bodies. He asked questions which would not be adequately answered until the late 1960s.

The Koryaks had known since time immemorial that, if consumed, the urine of a person who had eaten fly agaric produced powerful and long-lasting intoxicating effects. On one day a man might become moderately drunk on fly agarics "and by tomorrow may have completely slept off this moderate intoxication and be completely sober; but if he now drinks a cup of his own urine, he will become far more intoxicated than he was from the mushroom the day

Vladimir Jochelson, the Russian anthropologist, in a Yakut house during his expedition to study the role of the fly agaric in northern Siberia. His findings parallel those of R. Gordon Wasson in Middle America.

before. It is not at all uncommon, therefore, that drunkards who have consumed this poisonous mushroom will preserve their urine as if it were a precious liqueur and will drink it as the occasion offers ..." Because of this peculiar phenomenon, the tribesmen could prolong their ecstasy for up to a week with a relatively small number of fly agarics.

Von Langsdorf wondered not only about the psychopharmacologic aspects of the alkaloid in fly agaric, but also about whether there could be something about the mushroom that imparted a special, "possibly quite pleasant," smell and taste to urine. He concluded by saying that the nature of the fly agaric "offers the scientist, physician, and naturalist a great deal of food for thought; our *materia medica* [entire range of available medicines] might perhaps be enriched with one of the most efficacious remedies."

Though the very idea of drinking urine may be horrifying, one must recognize that Native American and Eastern

Jochelson and his crew on a crude raft on a Siberian river. They found that, while among the Chukchi and Koryak only men used the mushrooms, among other northeastern Siberian tribes women also indulged.

attitudes toward urine are very different from those prevailing in Western culture. In Asia, urine was widely employed as a medicine and as a sterile disinfectant, and in some places it served in religious ceremonies. Native American people of the Pacific Northwest, across from Siberia, felt that urine had magical, transformational, even life-restoring powers. The Kwakiutl of coastal British Columbia even identified urine as the miraculous "water of life" that, sprinkled over the bones of dead relatives, could magically restore them to life. But among these people no connection is known to have been made between mushrooms and urine.

The Chemistry and Psychopharmacology of Fly-Agaric Mushrooms

In 1869 the alkaloid muscarine was isolated from *A. muscaria*. First thought to be the main hallucinogenic agent in the fly agaric, it is now known to play a minor role in producing the mushroom's effects. Muscarine is related to choline, a

A Siberian Chukchi man with a wooden urine vessel. Tribesmen knew that ingesting the urine of someone who had recently eaten fly agaric would produce hallucinatory effects and thus extend mushroom intoxication.

vitamin of the B complex that is essential to the metabolism of fat, and when it is taken in very large doses (more than would be present in the usual dose of mushrooms), it can produce such decidedly unpleasant symptoms as profuse sweating, excessive salivation, uncontrollable twitching, abdominal colic (with involuntary evacuation of bowels and bladder), blurred vision, and respiratory depression.

Some twitching is indeed associated with fly-agaric intoxication, but the other adverse symptoms listed above are not. The symptoms of muscarine poisoning are inconsistent with the Siberian tribesmen's claims that inebriation from fly agaric is much more pleasant and benign than getting drunk on brandy, and that the aftereffects, if any, are more bearable. Clearly the positive psychoactive effects of the fly agaric cannot be attributed to muscarine. What then is responsible?

A team of Japanese scientists and University of Zurich professors Conrad H. Eugster and Peter G. Waser have isolated from the fly agaric various amino acid derivatives, most importantly the two compounds ibotenic acid and muscimol. These compounds produce effects identical to those reported by Siberian tribal peoples and others who have experimented with fly agaric. Subsequently, Swiss and Japanese scientists, working in collaboration, isolated two additional, though less important, psychoactive constituents.

Muscimol is the most important constituent. In addition to being a potent hallucinogen, it holds the key to both the urine-drinking custom and the preference for dried rather than fresh specimens. The investigators reported that muscimol passes through the kidneys in a basically unaltered form, which explains why intoxication results from drinking the urine of a mushroom eater. The scientists also noted that muscarine, with its unpleasant side effects, seems to be lacking in fly-agaric urine. The human body must be able to metabolize or degrade this compound.

Ibotenic acid, another principal ingredient, naturally converts to muscimol, a more stable compound. This relates directly to the way in which Siberian tribesmen customarily prepared fly agarics for consumption. By drying the mushrooms in the sun or over a fire, or by letting them dry in the ground, the ibotenic acid is transformed into muscimol, thereby producing more potent mushrooms.

The Great Lakes Chippewas, or Ojibways, are the only Native American people known to have discovered the fly agaric. They included it in their sacred pharmacopoeia and used it in their ecstatic divination.

CHAPTER 6

THE FLY AGARIC IN THE NEW WORLD

*B*ecause many Native American peoples included the ecstatic religious experience in their cultures, one would expect that their shamanistic rituals and psychological healing practices would have utilized the fly agaric. However, the evidence of the Indians' use of it is limited to only one area, the Great Lakes, and one people, the Algonquian-speaking Ojibway (known as Chippewa south of the U.S.-Canadian border). There have also been reports of the mushroom's use in northwestern Canada. This evidence does show that some Indians had discovered the fly agaric and its effects, had adopted it into their sacred pharmacopoeia and mythology, and had used it in their ecstatic divination.

In fact, the bark of the birch—the tree most favored by the fly agaric—was the most common multipurpose material used by Subarctic and Woodlands Indians from western Canada to the Atlantic. People searching in the forest for birch and making offerings to the spirits of the trees whose bark they removed could hardly have missed the beautiful mushrooms growing close by.

An Ojibway legend from Ontario tells the story of two brothers, Swift Current and Silver Cloud, who, in the days when the Ojibway were a proud and powerful nation, lived in a village near Lake Nipigon. One year the winter was especially long and hard, and the brothers set out to find deer to feed their starving people. After many hours they managed to wound only a single deer, which led them on an arduous pursuit and then, leaping over a huge boulder, finally vanished. On the other side of the boulder the brothers discovered a tunnel that led to a beautiful green meadow teeming with bright red mushrooms.

Though Swift Current was afraid, Silver Cloud only laughed at his brother's apprehension, picked some of the red mushrooms, and put them into his mouth. At once he experienced a feeling of peace and calm and invited his brother to join him in the pleasures of the mushrooms. But as he spoke he was transformed into a bright red mushroom.

Frightened, Swift Current ran to find help and, once again in the wintry world they had left behind, he found the powerful Bear Shaman who gave him a doeskin medicine bag and a magic arrow. He told Swift Current to hunt an eagle and fill the bag with magic sand. Then he was to return to the otherworld, pick the mushroom that was his brother, return to this world, plant it in the snow, and sprinkle it with the sacred sand.

Swift Current followed the great shaman's instructions and when he sprinkled the magical sand over the mushroom, his brother changed back into human form.

The red mushroom figures in other Ojibway legends, but also survives in Ojibway shamanism as more than just myth. Recently, the sacred use of the hallucinogenic mushroom was linked to an ancient annual ceremony practiced by some Ojibway on Lake Superior. An isolated case of Native American use of A. muscaria has also been reported from northwestern Canada, where shamans of the Dogrib (an Athapascan-speaking people living on the Mackenzie mountain range) are said to include this mushroom as a sacrament in the ritual initiation of neophyte healers.

In Mexico and Central America, some of the Maya Indians associated this mushroom with supernatural forces controlling weather phenomena, especially lightning bolts. However, there is no evidence that it was used as a divine inebriant. In Quiche Maya, a language spoken by hundreds of thousands of Indians in the Guatemalan highlands, the fly agaric is known as *kakulja*, the pre-Hispanic name of the god of the lightning bolt. And the Tzeltal-speaking Maya call it *yuy chauk*, which also means mushroom of the lightning bolt. No one knows why this association was made. Though perhaps the fly agaric was once associated with a powerful and well-loved divinity, today it is feared and avoided.

Amanita and the Counter-Culture

By the end of the 1970s hallucinogenic mushrooms had become a recreational drug in the United States and Canada. In many American cities *A. muscaria* mushrooms were being sold for $200 a pound. One health food store in Toronto was even selling them over-the-counter at $15 an ounce, and sales were reported as being "brisk" with "favorable reports from users."

A Mayan stele discovered by Guatemalan banana planters after it had been buried beneath the jungle for centuries. Mayan Indians associated fly agaric with the lightning bolt, an association reflected in their name for this fungi, kakulja, *the pre-Hispanic word used for the god of lightning. Though perhaps in the past this mushroom was connected with a powerful and well-loved divinity, today it is greatly feared and avoided by the Indians.*

This represents a dramatic switch from the public's previous conception of the mushroom. In 1927, for example, a Canadian Government handbook on the common edible and poisonous fungi of Canada classified the fly agaric as "deadly poisonous ... one of our most poisonous species" that is "unfortunately widely distributed." The same official publication declared *A. muscaria* and *A. phalloides* to be the two species most responsible for mushroom poisoning in that country.

This misconception continued to be disseminated. A more recent, official handbook, *Edible and Poisonous Mushrooms of Canada*, published in 1962, again characterized the fly agaric as being "deadly poisonous," and it called *A. pantherina* a "very poisonous mushroom" that has "caused more deaths in Europe than *A. muscaria*."

These judgments, unsupported by hard scientific evidence, are echoed to varying degrees by virtually every mushroom handbook in the English language. Nevertheless, on some people these official works seem to have made less of an impression than have the writings of the Wassons on the Siberian mushroom cults (1957), R. Gordon Wasson's more recent work on *A. muscaria*, and personal experiences. These people who continue to use psychoactive mushrooms have apparently disregarded the well-founded warnings that where *any* wild mushrooms are concerned, detailed knowledge and discretion are essential.

According to Jonathan Ott, a research chemist well acquainted with the field of psychoactive fungi, fly agaric is now one of the most widely used hallucinogenic mushrooms in the United States. *A. pantherina* is not far behind, at least in the Pacific Northwest, where users are said to prefer it to fly agaric because of its greater potency.

Considering the bad publicity that *A. pantherina* has received, it is interesting to note that in the Pacific Northwest some people have long used this mushroom as food rather than as a means of achieving altered states of consciousness. To prepare them for the table or for canning, the mushroom caps are peeled and then parboiled. Because the psychoactive toxins are water-soluble, this method, passed from generation to generation, removes these chemicals from *A. pantherina*. It is possible that the mushroom eaters are not even aware that the species contains the toxins.

Despite the many reports of positive mushroom experiences, there are cases of accidental "poisoning." Interestingly, these cases demonstrate the marked differences between the experiences and perceptions of intentional and unintentional ingesters. Ott interviewed 24 people who had consumed *Amanitas*, 9 of whom had done so accidentally, each on a single occasion. The intentional users had had a total of 280 experiences, 11 having used the mushrooms from 1 to 3 times, while the remaining 4 had taken the fungus from 12 to 200 times.

Of the 9 people who had ingested the mushroom accidentally, 7 found the experience intensely unpleasant, and 4 of them had felt that they were dying. One of the accidental users did not initially connect the effects with a mushroom, and never feared death, but found the hallucinations frightening. Three reported nausea and 7 reported drowsiness, 5

An Ojibway medicine man of the Bunji tribe in Manitoba, Canada. An Ojibway legend describes how an ancient shaman revealed to them the secrets of the magic mushroom.

of whom eventually lost consciousness. In general, these people had very negative feelings about mushrooms and did not understand why anyone would intentionally ingest them.

In contrast, all 15 of the intentional users found the experience to be pleasurable. Some of them described it as being unique, while others noted similarities to LSD, marijuana, peyote, and/or mushrooms containing psilocybin. Only 1 member of this group reported muscle spasms. Though 3 of the 15 intentional users became drowsy, none lost consciousness. All of them experienced varying degrees of hallucinations, but none of them was perceived as being unpleasant or frightening.

Ott concluded that the fear of death and the unpleasant effects so often reported by those who accidentally ingested

Richard E. Schultes (left), internationally known botanist specializing in hallucinogenic, medicinal, and poisonous plants, examining a Cannabis indica *plant, a variety of marijuana, during a research trip to Afghanistan.*

the mushrooms "result from the fear of mushrooms which pervades our culture. Because of their childhood training, upon the onset of the subjective effects these users typically felt that they had eaten deadly poisonous mushrooms, and hence were in peril of their lives .... It is hard to imagine how such persons, with this attitude, could conceivably have enjoyed the experience."

In addition to the subjectivity of a user's perceptions, there is great variability in the toxicity of the *Amanita* species and their varieties, and in an individual's tolerance to toxins within the mushrooms. Because of this, one must be very cautious about eating one of them even when there seems to be no doubt that the mushroom in question is not a highly poisonous species but the fly agaric.

Some people who have accidentally eaten hallucinogenic mushrooms have had terrifying experiences, sometimes including the sensation of dying and hallucinations of figures such as those illustrated in The House of Death, *a painting by Jakob von Wyl.*

A stone carving from Guatemala of a mushroom anthropomorphized as a seated human figure with a mushroom cap on its head. Figures such as this, which began to surface in the 1800s, have been associated with traditional native mushroom cults dating back more than 2000 years.

CHAPTER 7

THE MAGIC MUSHROOMS OF INDIAN AMERICA

*I*n the late 1800s a curious type of stone artifact began turning up in Central America, mostly in the highlands and on the Pacific mountain slope of Guatemala. They were all shaped like mushrooms, though some were simple representations and others were more complex—their stems merging with carved human or animal effigies. In 1898 a German geographer, Carl Sapper, described some of these unusual artifacts and suggested that they might be mushroom deities. Why gods should be depicted as mushrooms he did not ask, nor at that time was there much interest in the subject.

Today approximately 300 of these curious artifacts have been found. Though most were found in Guatemala, some were discovered as far south as Honduras and El Salvador, and as far north as southern and western Mexico. Many of them are now known to date to the 1st millenium B.C.E., and others may have been created as late as the last centuries before the Spanish Conquest (16th century). Except for a group of nine beautifully carved miniatures found in a tomb near Guatemala City, the objects average 12 inches to 15 inches in height. For several reasons the miniature sculptures are quite remarkable. Not only does their number correspond to the well-known Maya conception of a nine-level underworld, but the nine mushroom effigies were found with nine equally diminutive *metates* (grinding stones) and *manos* (stone rollers used with the grinding stones). At first this coincidence may seem extraordinary, but discoveries made in the Mexican countryside have solved the mystery.

Indian Mushrooms and Spanish Devils

Until the early 1950s, when the Wassons began to focus on the ancient mushroom cults of pre-Columbian Central America, scholars were not asking the correct questions about the mushroom stones. Why did the ancient people expend so much time and skill on stone effigies? Why were they sometimes associated with such animals as jaguars and toads, or with human figures? For some reason Sapper's idea that the mushroom stones represented pagan deities was forgotten. Even more curious, the scholars failed to make an association between the mushroom sculptures and the ritual use of inebriating mushrooms by the Aztecs, described by 16th-century Spanish friars. In fact, early American colonial sources state that such mushrooms were venerated and widely used in the divinatory rituals of some Native American peoples.

A stone effigy (c. 400 B.C.E.) of a seated jaguar with a mushroom growing from its back, discovered at the ancient ceremonial center of Kaminaljuyu, near Guatemala City.

The Wassons, however, assumed that the mushroom sculptures *were* connected to the mushroom cults reported by the Spanish chroniclers. When in 1952 they came to Mexico for the first time, they were surprised that this association was seen as being new and revolutionary. Stephan de Borhegyi, a specialist in Guatemalan archaeology, readily accepted the Wassons' theory and immediately began to classify all the mushroom stones. By doing so he was able to demonstrate how they changed over time and prove that the early artifacts had been created prior to 100 B.C.E.

The most detailed description of early Aztec civilization was made by Bernadino de Sahagún, a Franciscan priest fluent in Nahuatl, the language of the Aztecs. He compiled a 12-volume work entitled *General History of the Things of New Spain*, also known as the *Florentine Codex*. Using methods similar to those of modern ethnographers, Sahagún formed a detailed picture of Aztec life, including the natural environment and the resources of ancient central Mexico. In his descriptions he several times mentioned sacred mushrooms—their taxonomy, their effects, and the different contexts in which they were used.

A clawed and beaked demon hovers over a stand of tawny mushrooms in a 16th-century illustration included in the Florentine Codex, *compiled by Franciscan priest and Spanish chronicler Bernadino de Sahagún.*

He speaks of mushrooms with small, rounded heads and slender stalks. The mushrooms were known as *teonanacatl*, from the word *teo*, meaning divine or marvelous, and *nacatl*, which means flesh or mushroom. An Aztec, after mixing the mushrooms with honey, would eat this preparation and then see "many things which make him afraid, or make him laugh."

Sahagún described the use of such mushrooms for producing ecstatic visions and divinations of the future. On a certain feast day the participants would consume the mushroom, and soon afterwards some would begin to dance and then weep, while others would merely sit and dream. Some mushroom users had visions of dying, of falling in battle, of being eaten by wild animals, or of becoming wealthy. Everything, good or bad, that might happen to a person could be revealed under the influence of the *teonanacatl*. When the effect had worn off, "they consulted among themselves and told one another what they had seen in visions."

An Aztec man eating mushrooms (lower right) while being watched by a supernatural being with a skeletal face and jaguar claws (Aztec codex).

In another 16th-century history of the Aztecs the Dominican priest Diego Durán wrote of inebriating mushrooms used outside of divinatory rituals. Mushrooms that "make a man lose his senses" were taken to solemnize the enthronement of Aztec rulers. The mushrooms, eaten raw, filled people with pleasure and made them lose their senses, as if "they had drunk a great quantity of wine.... With the strength of these mushrooms they saw visions and had revelations about the future, since the Devil spoke to them in their madness."

For Durán, as for other historians of his time, the Aztec gods were the creations of the Devil and his coconspirators. For example, Motolinía, a contemporary of his, saw only the Devil's own handiwork in the sacred mushrooms, which, he claimed, caused the Indians "to see a thousand visions, especially serpents, and as they would be out of their senses, it would seem to them that their legs and bodies were full of worms eating them alive." Though he called the mushrooms "flesh of god," the god was really "the Devil whom they worshipped." What made Motolinía particularly uncomfortable was the similarity he perceived between the Indian

The five regions of the Aztec world—the present world and the fire god, Ziutecuhtli, surrounded by the four previous worlds.

mushroom-eating ritual and the Christian Eucharist, a coincidence he likewise attributed to the Devil's influence.

However, though Durán felt it was his supreme duty to eradicate all vestiges of "idolatry," he also acknowledged the good and beautiful aspects of the old culture. He knew that, beneath the thin veneer of newly-imposed Christianity, the old religion and its rites continued to thrive.

The Trials of the Mushroom Users

The earliest mention of divine mushrooms is in the record of the trial of two Indian brothers in Mexico City in 1537, 16 years after the destruction of the Aztec capital. Because

A fresco of the Aztec rain god, Tlaloc, enthroned in his paradise of rain clouds above the paradise of blessed souls. In 1537 a Mexican Indian, who went by the name of Tlaloc, was tried for organizing his fellow Indians against the Spanish conquerors as well as for invoking the Indian gods, an offense for which he could have been tortured and burned at the stake.

of their native names—Mixcóatl, Cloud Serpent, who was the Aztec god of the hunt and personification of the Milky Way, and Tlaloc, an earth lord who was the god of rain— one can readily assume that the accused had once been Aztec priests. The presiding judge, Juan de Zumárraga, was a Franciscan priest who served as first bishop of the new colony that the conquerors called New Spain.

The charges were serious: the brothers were accused of organizing and arming their fellow Indians against the conquerors. They were also charged with invoking the Indian gods, an offense that was considered to be even worse since they had been baptized. Their use of sacred mushrooms was mentioned five times in the course of the proceedings. Indians—especially apostates—found guilty of such charges were usually tortured and then burned at the stake. In fact, the brothers got off relatively lightly, a mark of the essential humanity of Bishop Zumárraga.

The Spanish were determined to eliminate any vestige of the old religion. They were especially annoyed by the stubborn persistence of the veneration and ritual use of plant hallucinogens—the mushrooms, the seeds of the morning glory (*Turbina corymbosa*), the peyote cactus (*Lophophora williamsii*), and other psychoactive species. A century after the Conquest there was still no sign that the Spanish effort had met with any measurable success. Either the sacred hallucinogens of pre-Conquest times were used secretly or their use merged with the worship of the Christian saints.

Forced to acknowledge that idolatry persisted all around them, 17th-century clerics composed extensive manuals to alert their fellow ministers to the survival of pre-Christian practices. One such manual, written in 1629 by Hernando Ruíz de Alarcón, is unique in that it gives a complete account of the use and meaning of the sacred plant hallucinogens among the Indians of the Mexican states of Guerrero and Morelos. In addition, using the original Aztec language he recorded the chants, charms, and spells employed by Indian shamans to ward off evil, assure success, and cure everything from toothache to disorders of the urinary tract.

Another guide, written by Jacinto de la Serna, tells of one *curandero*, or curing shaman, named Juan Chichiton (John Little Dog), a "great master of superstitions," who committed "a great idolatry" with "mushrooms that are gathered in the uplands." This species, called *quautlan-nanacatl*, or forest mushroom, was gathered by native priests and old men, who, while in prayer and "superstitious entreaties," gathered the divine mushrooms all through the night, stopping only at dawn.

One day Juan Chichiton officiated at a gathering that honored a Catholic saint. The saint's image was placed on the altar, together with the mushrooms and a bowl of *pulque* (the fermented sap of the giant agave cactus, or century plant). After all-night singing to the sound of the *teponaztli* (a horizontal wooden drum made from a hollow log), Chichiton offered mushrooms to all those present, "in the manner of Communion, and pulque to drink." What with the mushrooms and the pulque, "all went out of their heads, a shame it was to see." De la Serna made every effort to apprehend and punish the offending Little Dog, but, he sadly admits, the *curandero* proved too clever and eluded the clutches of the Inquisition.

A polished red clay figure from Colima, Mexico, of a humpbacked dwarf holding a pair of peyote cactus plants. Dwarfs in Mexican Indian myths are usually associated with fertility and wealth.

"Mushroom of the Underworld"

During the colonial period Spanish priests in the highlands of Guatemala labored to compile dictionaries of the Mayan languages. Though the priests heard of no instances of mushroom use, the terms they collected make it clear that whether or not the Indians were then using psychoactive fungi, they were well acquainted with several species and their effects. For example, one of the earliest of the colonial word lists, the Vico dictionary, compiled before the middle of the 16th century, mentions a mushroom called *xibalbáj okóx. Xibalbáj* is translated as the nine-level Maya underworld, and *okóx* means mushroom. Therefore, *xibalbáj okóx* can be seen as meaning not only "mushroom of the underworld" but as mushroom that gives one visions of the land of the dead, or of the lords of the underworld.

This same intoxicating mushroom is also mentioned in a later word list, Tomas Coto's *Vocabulario de la lengua*

Detail from the Tlaloc fresco of a highly stylized morning glory plant with trumpet-shaped flowers pouring out streams of precious water.

Cakchiquel, (c. 1690). According to this dictionary, the mushroom of Xibalba was also known as *k'aizalah okóx*, which can be translated as "mushroom that makes one lose one's judgment." This dictionary also lists a species called *k'ekc'un*, which inebriates or makes one drunk, and yet another, *muxán okóx*, "mushroom that makes the eater crazy."

The Mushrooms Challenged

The cumulative evidence, then, was surely sufficient for some connection to be made between the Guatemalan mushroom effigies and the documented veneration of sacred mushrooms in Mexico before the Conquest and during colonial times. However, scholars still did not accept this. In the early part of this century there was even some opposition to the very idea that native mushroom species actually produced the psychoactive effects mentioned in the early colonial accounts.

Respected botanist William Safford insisted that morning glory seeds contained no psychoactive components and that the hallucinogenic mushrooms described in Aztec chronicles were actually peyote. Research has since proved him wrong.

The distinguished American botanist William A. Safford, a respected scientist and an expert on some of the psychoactive flora of the North American Indians, was one of the most vocal opponents of the belief in the existence of hallucinogenic mushrooms. Safford also did not accept the testimony of numerous Spanish colonial sources on the subject of *ololiuhqui*, the Aztec name for the potent hallucinogenic morning glory seeds.

In his 1920 monograph on the *Daturas* (the genus of plants that includes the jimsonweed, a plant that contains psychoactive compounds) of the Old and New Worlds, Safford insisted that because no psychoactive compounds had ever been found in any of the Convolvulaceae (the order of plants that includes the morning glories), the real *ololiuhqui* could only have been a species of the genus *Datura*. Several *Daturas* were indeed among the sacred hallucinogenic and medicinal plants in the herbal pharmacopoeia of the Aztecs, and their toxicity and psychoactive effects were well known and documented. Safford was, however, completely wrong. The Aztec priests and physicians did use *Datura* as medicine *and* as an ecstasy-producing stimulant, but *ololiuhqui* was not the Aztec name for their seeds.

Young peyote cactus plants collected from the desert in northern Mexico. The hallucinogenic peyote "buttons," the sun-dried crowns of the plants, have been discovered in Texas and dated as being approximately 1000 years old.

Five years earlier Safford had insisted that, despite everything the Spanish chroniclers and the Aztecs had said, *teonanacatl* was probably nothing other than the peyote cactus, whose dried and shriveled "buttons" had been mistaken for mushroom caps. "Three centuries of investigation," Safford wrote, "have failed to reveal an endemic fungus used as an intoxicant in Mexico, nor is such a fungus mentioned either in works on mycology or pharmacography [writings on drugs and medicine]; yet the belief prevails even now that there is a narcotic Mexican fungus."

In fact, there had not been three centuries of investigation, for after the initial flurry of interest in intoxicating mushrooms, and the colonizers' attempts to suppress mushroom use in the 1st century after the Conquest, the topic disappears from the literature, and does not reappear until the first half of the 20th century. Safford was a good botanist, but in this case he, like so many others, stubbornly dismissed the observations and knowledge of Europeans, Mexicans, and Native Americans.

Safford's arguments were published many years before the distinguished Swiss chemist, Albert Hofmann, identified the alkaloids that give the Mexican mushrooms their extraordinary effects, and before he discovered that morning glories and LSD contain similar hallucinogenic compounds. During the past 30 years the scholarly research into the Mexican hallucinogens, mushrooms included, has been filled with hunches, clues, false leads, and painstaking scientific detection, not unlike a good detective story. Hofmann's role in that developing tale has proved to be crucial. With his discovery of LSD on the eve of World War II, the modern research into consciousness-transforming drugs rapidly escalated.

An Austrian Pioneer

Blas Pablo Reko, an Austrian-born engineer and ethnobotanist who worked in Mexico a half century ago, was certain that the old accounts about morning glories and mushrooms were correct. In 1919 he had collected samples of small seeds called *ololuc* from Oaxacan Indian shamans and identified them as the seeds of the morning glory. At the same time he heard persistent reports that intoxicating mushrooms, called *teonanacatl* by the Aztecs, were still being used in divinatory rituals. But then, in 1922, N.L. Britton and J.N. Rose published their classic work, *The Cactaceae*, in which they quoted Safford's identification of *teonanacatl* as peyote. This prompted a letter from Reko, in which he insisted that Safford was "surely wrong," and that the mushroom known to the Aztecs as "god's flesh" was still very much in religious use under the same old name by the Indians of the Sierra Juarez in Oaxaca. But at the time the significance of Reko's observation seems to have escaped his fellow scholars.

Rediscovery of a Living Mushroom Rite

In 1936 another distinguished ethnologist, Roberto J. Weitlaner, was able to collect some of the "magic mushrooms" while visiting Mazatec Indians in Oaxaca. He sent them to Reko, who forwarded them to the Botanical Museum of Harvard University. Unfortunately, they arrived too badly deteriorated to permit identification.

In 1938 Weitlaner was again among the Mazatecs, in the village of Huautla de Jiménez, far from mainstream Mexican society. He and his coworkers were the first outsiders

Mazatec Indian girls in the mountains of Oaxaca, Mexico, display handfuls of freshly picked psilocybin mushrooms. Mazatec shamans now invoke both their gods and the Christian god in their mushroom rituals.

permitted to attend an all-night curing ritual in which intoxicating mushrooms were consumed by the officiating shaman. The ritual was described to a scholarly gathering in Mexico City in 1938—the first such account since the time of the early Spanish writers. Though in the intervening centuries the Indians had adapted their ancient ritual to Christianity, not only Christian deities and saints were invoked in the mushroom ritual, but also the supernatural "masters" (*dueños* or *duendes* in Mexican Spanish) of mountains, rivers, thunder, rocks, earth, stars, sun, moon, and plants. In some cases the Mazatecs used not only the sacred mushrooms but morning glory seeds as well.

The First Mushrooms Identified

A month after Weitlaner's experience, Reko and Richard Evans Schultes, a young Harvard biologist who would later become the director of the Harvard Botanical Museum and an authority on New World plant hallucinogens, began doing research in the same region. At Huautla de Jiménez they secured samples of hallucinogenic mushrooms together with information about their use. The new specimens were properly preserved and identified at Harvard as *Panaeolus campanulatus* of the variety *sphinctrinus* Bresadola.

In 1939 Schultes published the first scientific description of the "magic mushrooms" of Oaxaca. Two years later in a definitive monograph he identified the *ololiuhqui* as the much-venerated hallucinogenic seeds of the morning glory. Subsequently, one of the samples collected by Schultes and Reko was identified as *Stropharia cubensis* Earle, a species first found and described in 1904 by F. S. Earle in Cuba. Today some mycologists identify it not as a separate genus but as a member of *Psilocybes*.

Despite the early ethnographic evidence that supported the existence of the *Panaeolus* mushroom's hallucinogenic properties, it took three more decades before a systematic study of this genus was published. Only then was it shown that although some species are psychoactive, others of the same genus are not. Eventually other kinds of psychoactive mushrooms were discovered in Mexico by the Wassons and their collaborators, and by other investigators, so that now a substantial literature exists on these extraordinary fungi.

The Toltec Indian creation myth also served as a guide for male initiation rites, which included purification with hot water followed by a journey through the "seven hells of divine language."

The Sacred Mushrooms of Mexico

In 1952, during their research into the worldwide history of mushroom cults, the Wassons first learned of the early Spanish descriptions of Mexican mushroom rites and the ethnobotanists' and ethnologists' confirmations. They were already acquainted with some of the Guatemalan mushroom stones. In early 1953 Wasson received a letter from Eunice V. Pike, a Protestant missionary and linguist who had spent years with the Mazatec Indians in Mexico. In it she described the intermingling of pre-Christian and Christian religious concepts and terminologies in Mazatec divinatory mushroom rituals. The Mazatecs even identified their sacred mushroom with Christ, from whose blood the mushrooms had sprung and whose voice it was that spoke through the mushrooms to people seeking their advice.

Other Mexican Indian peoples besides the Mazatecs venerated the sacred mushrooms, calling them the "little saints" and supernatural masters and mistresses of the divine earth. Thus, for the Mixe, one of the most isolated and traditional of the Indian peoples of mountainous southern Mexico, the mushrooms were *los señores*, the lords, or, in their native tongue, *nwintson'ahtom nashwin mush*, "our Masters, the Mushrooms of the [Holy] World." By "world" the Mixe meant the life-giving earth, which was perceived as

A controversial 13th-century Romanesque fresco of the temptation of Eve in the Garden of Eden. The Tree of Knowledge, entwined by a serpent, bears a striking resemblance to the fly agaric.

a male/female deity of equal stature with Christ and the Virgin Mary. Thus, the mushrooms were revered and respected as supernatural earth beings, which were sometimes male, sometimes female, and endowed with speech, will, and divine knowledge.

The Wassons made their first foray into the Mazatec mushroom world in 1953. Accompanied by Roberto Weitlaner, they attended a mushroom *velada* (vigil) in Huautla de Jiménez and watched the officiating shaman consume the mushrooms while smoking the powerful native Indian tobacco to reinforce his divinatory powers and please the spirits. Two years later Wasson witnessed a somewhat different divinatory session in which the shaman—in this case the famous María Sabina—ingested the mushroom and invited the scientist to do likewise. And so, on a summer night in 1955, Wasson and his companion, Alan Richardson, became the first outsiders to consume the sacred mushroom and be directly drawn into an ancient ecstatic Indian ritual that had successfully evaded detection in previous centuries and had survived into modern times. It was an unforgettable experience, Wasson later wrote, one that was to profoundly affect and guide the future research of one who for many years had been unable to think of mushrooms as anything but "repulsive parasites."

An early Greek mosaic of Jesus. The Mazatec Indians of Mexico believe that the sacred mushrooms spring from the blood of Jesus and that it is his voice that speaks in the hallucinatory rituals.

A few days later Wasson's wife, Valentina, and daughter Masha joined him in Huautla. Wasson participated in a second session of the mushroom ritual on July 2, 1955, and on July 5 Valentina and Masha became, so far as is known, the first white people to eat Mexican "magic mushrooms" experimentally—removed from the native ceremonial setting. Their experience was pleasant, full of nostalgic visions, without nausea, and without any aftereffects—an experience far different from the terrifying apparitions Motolonia ascribed to the mushrooms in the 16th century.

Over the next several years, Wasson took mushrooms both experimentally and within the context of the ritual Indian settings. He also made the acquaintance of shamans from other Indian groups, including Nahuatl (Aztec), Mixtec, Mixe, and Zapotec, and from them learned details of their own ecstatic experiences, liturgies, and techniques.

It was during a visit to Juxtlahuaca, in the mountainous country of the Mixtec Indians, that Wasson first saw the method of ingesting the mushrooms in liquid form. In addition, it was then that the symbolic meaning of the stone mushroom on whose stem was depicted a barebreasted

Pioneer ethnomycologist R. Gordon Wasson identified the ancient Vedic deity Soma as fly agaric, authored numerous works on the sacred roles of psychoactive mushrooms, and was the first outsider to take part in an ancient ecstatic Mexican mushroom ritual. He is seen here with a pre-Columbian clay sculpture from Veracruz, Mexico, depicting a priestess of the sacred mushroom.

woman using a *mano* and *metate* suddenly became clear. On the night of July 5–6, 1960, he attended a Mixtec *velada* in which he saw a young girl using a *mano* to grind the sacred mushrooms into pulp on a stone *metate*. This, it turned out, is considered a religious office, which can be filled only by a *doncella*, a maiden. Wasson's experience in Juxtlahuaca also helped explain the symbolism of the nine miniature *metates* and *manos* found in association with the nine little mushroom stones in a Guatemalan tomb.

Despite his enthusiasm for the extraordinary psychic effects of the mushrooms and other sacred plant hallucinogens, Wasson was careful to point out that there were many other means of attaining ecstatic religious visions. Clearly, poets, prophets, mystics, and ascetics, he wrote, have experienced visions without recourse to psychotropic substances. Nevertheless, "the advantage of the mushrooms is that it puts many within reach of this state without having to suffer the mortifications of Blake or St. John. It permits you to see, more clearly than our perishing mortal eye can see, vistas beyond the horizons of this life."

The Quest for "Chemical Nirvanas"

In 1957 Wasson's description of what he had experienced in Huautla de Jiménez appeared in the pages of *Life* magazine. His article prompted a veritable avalanche of foreign pilgrims on the unsuspecting Indians of the Sierra Mazateca. Among them were serious students of the mushroom phenomenon but a much greater number of them were thrill seekers, self-styled students of the mind, "flower children," journalists, and people searching for psychic enlightenment, many of them looking for instant "chemical Nirvanas." Needless to say, their arrival greatly disrupted the relative peace and tranquility of traditional Indian life.

In her autobiography Maria Sabina recalled visits from "the young people with long hair" who came to her "in search of God," but didn't respect the Indian customs, eating the sacred mushrooms wherever and whenever they liked. Never were the sainted mushrooms "eaten with such a lack of respect," she remembered with great sadness. She felt that it was this profanation that had caused them to lose their ancient force and their sacred purity. In addition, it also brought about the intervention of the Mexican federal and state authorities in her native village and contributed to the legal strictures on trade in and use of the native hallucinogens.

The Active Ingredients in the Mexican Mushrooms

Just what causes the extraordinary effects of the sacred mushrooms of Mexico was a question to which Roger Heim, a leading French mycologist, addressed himself in his Paris laboratory. While he succeeded in propagating a laboratory culture of *Psilocybe mexicana*, the species most widely used by Indians, attempts to isolate the active principles had only limited success. In 1957 Heim submitted dried specimens of *P. mexicana* and other species to Hofmann for analysis at Sandoz Ltd., in Basel, Switzerland. With sufficient

Maria Sabina, a Mexican shaman, or a priest who uses magic for religious or healing purposes, is seen here (top) chanting during a sacred ritual and (below) giving the final benediction. Sabina believed that eating sacred mushrooms allowed her to have contact with the other world and thereby gain hidden knowledge.

samples at hand, Hofmann isolated the alkaloidal compounds and tested them on cats and dogs. The results were disappointingly inconclusive. The animals' subjective experiences could not be determined.

Hofmann then decided to ingest the mushrooms himself. Beginning a half hour after he had consumed 2.4 gm of dried pieces—equivalent to a medium dose by Indian standards—and for the next six hours, he found his senses strangely and powerfully affected. The exterior world, he reported, "began to undergo a strange transformation. Everything assumed a Mexican character." Hofmann was well aware that this was caused by his knowledge of the mushroom's origin, but he was unable to shut out Mexican images. Thus, he "saw only Mexican motifs and colors." The attending physician, who regularly came to check Hofmann's pulse "was transformed into an Aztec priest."

A seriously ill, seventeen-year-old boy during two phases of a **Velada,** *or night vigil, performed by* **Maria Sabina.** *After the boy ate the mushrooms (left), Sabina made a diagnosis based on his reaction to the sacred plant. Several hours later, the boy, upon hearing Sabina's prognosis—that there was no hope for recovery—collapsed.*

At the peak of the intoxication, about 90 minutes after ingestion, "the rush of interior pictures, mostly abstract motifs rapidly changing in shape and color, reached such an alarming degree that I feared that I would be torn into this whirlpool of form and color and would dissolve." When the effects wore off, Hofmann felt his return to everyday reality was "a happy return from a strange, fantastic but quite real world to an old and familiar home."

Hofmann and his coworkers identified the principal active agent as an organic compound related to serotonin, a neurotransmitter (a chemical that carries signals from nerve to nerve) naturally present in the brain. He named the newly discovered hallucinogen psilocybin, after the most important plant genus in which it occurs. Also present in the mushroom is an unstable compound he called psilocin. Other scientists, including Americans V. E. Tyler and R. G. Benedict, analyzed several more New World and Old World species of *Psilocybe*. In addition, related species, none known to be employed in divinatory or shamanistic ritual, were analyzed. They too were found to contain the same psychoactive alkaloids.

After eating Psilocybe mexicana, *Swiss chemist Albert Hofmann, who first identified the hallucinogen psilocybin, feared he would dissolve in a whirlpool of form and color. In Hoffman's vision the doctor supervising the experiment was suddenly transformed into an Aztec priest.*

Once these compounds had been isolated from the mushroom, Hofmann's coworkers were able to prepare larger quantities of psilocybin and psilocin from sclerotia-containing mycelia of *P. mexicana*. (A sclerotium is a hardened mass of mycelium that, stored with reserve nutrients, remains dormant until there is a favorable opportunity for growth). With these larger amounts of the psychedelic compounds it became possible to determine the precise chemical structures of the compounds. And with this knowledge the hallucinogens could be synthesized, or prepared from raw chemicals.

The active ingredients of the sacred mushrooms, Hofmann reported, amount to approximately 0.03% of the total weight of the organism. This means that to achieve the same effects produced by 30 mushrooms a person would require only 0.01 gm of the crystallized powder. Obviously the human body is quite sensitive to these psychedelic compounds.

The Mushroom Alkaloids and Brain Chemistry

In a 1964 paper Hofmann summarized the results of his investigation of the sacred mushrooms. Most importantly, he

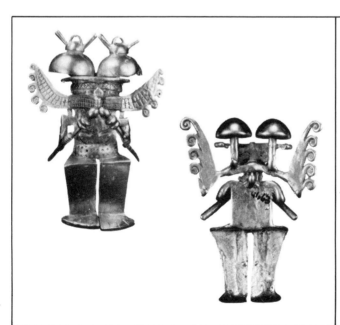

Pre-Columbian gold pectorals from Colombia, South America, with pairs of mushrooms on top of the heads, suggest that an early Indian culture may have made religious use of indigenous species of hallucinogenic fungi.

noted that psilocybin's and psilocin's chemical and structural relationship to serotonin provides an explanation for their psychic effects and offers insights into the chemistry of the brain itself. The pharmacological phenomena are explainable in terms of central excitation of the sympathetic nervous system. This part of the nervous system produces a heightened state of alertness, excitement, and alarm.

In human subjects, doses of 6 mg to 20 mg (milligrams) produce very minor physical symptoms, though they do bring about fundamental changes of consciousness, such as different perceptions of space and time, and an altered sense of one's psychological and physical self. One's sense of sight and hearing are greatly heightened, to such an extent that often visions and hallucinations occur. Not uncommonly, long-forgotten events, often going back to earliest childhood, may resurface with extraordinary clarity.

Ecology and Distribution of Psilocybe *Mushrooms*

The genus *Psilocybe* occurs on all continents of the world. It is found in Greenland and in South America's remote point at Tierra del Fuego, in virgin rain forests and gardens, on sugar cane refuse, and on mosses near the snowline. Though all species are not hallucinogenic, the psychedelic forms have been found everywhere.

Mexico alone contains 32 of the hallucinogenic members; Central and South America, including the Caribbean region, 26; Canada and the United States 18; Australasia 13; Asia (mainly in Japan) 9; Europe 8; and Africa, in Morocco and Algeria, 1. The tropical zones probably contain more unknown species, though with the unfortunate and rapid destruction of the tropical rain forests of the world, many species of these may disappear before they can be identified and studied.

Unlike the fly agaric, none of the *Psilocybe* are known to be parasitic or mycorrhizic. Rather, all species are saprophytic and derive their nutrients from clayey, sandy, muddy, or swampy soils; rotten wood or wood debris dispersed within the soil; tree stumps; herbaceous stems; humus; rich soils and soils covered by mosses; bogs; refuse materials, including paper; sugar cane debris; and dung.

A tropical rain forest, probably the environment in which many still-unidentified hallucinogenic mushrooms thrive. Because all over the world the effects of civilization are directly or indirectly destroying such forests, many mushroom species may be wiped out before they have been studied and their benefits to all life understood and appreciated.

MUSHROOM CAP

MORNING GLORY TENDRIL

TOBACCO FLOWER

MORNING GLORY FLOWER

SINICUICHE BUD

PSILOCYBE CAP

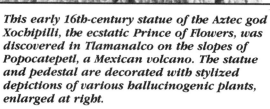

This early 16th-century statue of the Aztec god Xochipilli, the ecstatic Prince of Flowers, was discovered in Tlamanalco on the slopes of Popocatepetl, a Mexican volcano. The statue and pedestal are decorated with stylized depictions of various hallucinogenic plants, enlarged at right.

CHAPTER 8

PSILOCYBE USE IN THE UNITED STATES

*I*n recent years a considerable number of psychoactive species of *Psilocybe* have been identified in the United States, some not previously described or named elsewhere. Not surprisingly, word of their use in religious rituals in Mexico, like the published stories about the fly agaric in Siberian tribal culture, led to their recreational use in nonreligious settings. Recreational use of hallucinogenic mushrooms increased dramatically during the 1970s, and there is no reason to think that it is any less popular in the 1980s. This widespread use occurred in spite of the mushroom's inclusion in the list of illegal "mind-altering" substances.

Today the most serious problem with the recreational use of hallucinogenic mushrooms in the United States is the ignorance of the user. As mycologist Jonathan Ott noted in an overview of the mushroom phenomenon in the United States, the recent past has seen the emergence of an entirely new breed of mushroom hunters, many of them unable "to distinguish a bolete [a fungus of the Boletaceae family] from a morel." Unfortunately, a great deal of the published information on which these people have relied for guidance has been false or misleading. These unsophisticated users are exposing themselves to serious or even fatal health risks.

It should be emphasized that it is not true that any mushroom that turns blue when scratched or bruised, or any mushroom that grows on dung, is necessarily safe and/or hallucinogenic. Some young people are willing to ingest any kind of mushroom in the hope that one or another might be hallucinogenic. As a result newspapers have reported cases of poisoning and hospitalization from the recreational use of mushrooms incorrectly labeled hallucinogenic.

P. cubensis, relatively abundant, and consequently widely used, in the hot and humid Gulf states, is also popular on the Pacific coast and other parts of the country. Apparently the favorite of collectors in the Pacific Northwest is *P. semilanceata*, a species small in size but high in psilocybin content. This mushroom was once thought to be limited to Europe but is now known to occur not only in Oregon and Washington but also in British Columbia and the northeastern United States.

One previously unknown, and now reportedly popular, hallucinogenic species of *Psilocybe* in the Pacific Northwest owes its discovery to students at the University of Washington in Seattle. In 1973 they found it growing in cedar-bark mulch on their campus. Risking its possibly dangerous side effects, they nonetheless ingested it to test for psychoactive qualities. Subsequently, this mushroom, confirmed as being a new species, was labeled *P. stuntzii* Guzmán and Ott.

To what degree expectations influence effects is demonstrated by the case of *Gymnopilus spectabilis*, a common red-brown mushroom that grows on rotting or buried wood. Though very bitter-tasting, it is classified as nonpoisonous. In the 1960s it gained a wholly undeserved reputation as a hallucinogenic mushroom, though in fact it does not contain psilocybin or any other psychoactive compound. Nevertheless, because those who ingested the mushroom expected to experience hallucinations and the other psychedelic effects, they did in fact become high. This is reminiscent of anecdotes about persons in the 1960s who vehemently insisted that they had experienced LSD-like effects after ingesting the inner scrapings of banana peels.

Before psilocybin and psilocin were made illegal, pure, synthetic psilocybin was available in the United States as a pharmaceutical drug. But after their legal status changed and they were forced underground to became part of the black market, the purity and authenticity of these drugs came into question. Of 333 samples of street "psilocybin" or "Psilocybin mushrooms" analyzed by Pharm Chem Laboratories of Palo Alto, California, 25% were inert, or had no psychoactive qualities at all; 53% contained LSD; 1% contained PCP;

APPENDIX 2

STATE AGENCIES FOR THE PREVENTION AND TREATMENT OF DRUG ABUSE

ALABAMA

Department of Mental Health
Division of Mental Illness and
   Substance Abuse Community
   Programs
200 Interstate Park Drive
P.O. Box 3710
Montgomery, AL 36193
(205) 271-9253

ALASKA

Department of Health and Social
   Services
Office of Alcoholism and Drug
   Abuse
'ouch H-05-F
ıneau, AK 99811
ʻ)7) 586-6201

tially fatal effects

ARKANSAS

Department of Human Services
Office on Alcohol and Drug Abuse
   Prevention
1515 West 7th Avenue
Suite 310
Little Rock, AR 72202
(501) 371-2603

CALIFORNIA

Department of Alcohol and Drug
   Abuse
111 Capitol Mall
Sacramento, CA 95814
(916) 445-1940

COLORADO

Department of Health
Alcohol and Drug Abuse Division
4210 East 11th Avenue
Denver, CO 80220
ʻ320-6137

*A pair of pre-Co
painted polychrome tomb figures
from Jalisco, Mexico. The male
figure typically has a pair of
mushroom-like ornaments on
his head and is playing a
drum, the holy instrument
of the shamans.*

109

DISTRICT OF COLUMBIA
Department of Human Services
Office of Health Planning and
   Development
601 Indiana Avenue, NW
Suite 500
Washington, D.C. 20004
(202) 724-5641

FLORIDA
Department of Health and
   Rehabilitative Services
Alcoholic Rehabilitation Program
1317 Winewood Boulevard
Room 187A
Tallahassee, FL 32301
(904) 488-0396

Department of Health and
   Rehabilitative Services
Drug Abuse Program
1317 Winewood Boulevard
Building 6, Room 155
Tallahassee, FL 32301
(904) 488-0900

GEORGIA
Department of Human Resources
Division of Mental Health and
   Mental Retardation
Alcohol and Drug Section
618 Ponce De Leon Avenue, NE
Atlanta, GA 30365-2101
(404) 894-4785

HAWAII
Department of Health
Mental Health Division
Alcohol and Drug Abuse Branch
1250 Punch Bowl Street
P.O. Box 3378
Honolulu, HI 96801
(808) 548-4280

IDAHO
Department of Health and Welfare
Bureau of Preventive Medicine
Substance Abuse Section
450 West State
Boise, ID 83720
(208) 334-4368

ILLINOIS
Department of Mental Health and
   Developmental Disabilities
Division of Alcoholism
160 North La Salle Street
Room 1500
Chicago, IL 60601
(312) 793-2907

Illinois Dangerous Drugs
   Commission
300 North State Street
Suite 1500
Chicago, IL 60610
(312) 822-9860

INDIANA
Department of Mental Health
Division of Addiction Services
429 North Pennsylvania Street
Indianapolis, IN 46204
(317) 232-7816

IOWA
Department of Substance Abuse
505 5th Avenue
Insurance Exchange Building
Suite 202
Des Moines, IA 50319
(515) 281-3641

KANSAS
Department of Social Rehabilitation
Alcohol and Drug Abuse Services
2700 West 6th Street
Biddle Building
Topeka, KS 66606
(913) 296-3925

KENTUCKY
Cabinet for Human Resources
Department of Health Services
Substance Abuse Branch
275 East Main Street
Frankfort, KY 40601
(502) 564-2880

LOUISIANA
Department of Health and Human
    Resources
Office of Mental Health and
    Substance Abuse
655 North 5th Street
P.O. Box 4049
Baton Rouge, LA 70821
(504) 342-2565

MAINE
Department of Human Services
Office of Alcoholism and Drug
    Abuse Prevention
Bureau of Rehabilitation
32 Winthrop Street
Augusta, ME 04330
(207) 289-2781

MARYLAND
Alcoholism Control Administration
201 West Preston Street
Fourth Floor
Baltimore, MD 21201
(301) 383-2977

State Health Department
Drug Abuse Administration
201 West Preston Street
Baltimore, MD 21201
(301) 383-3312

MASSACHUSETTS
Department of Public Health
Division of Alcoholism
755 Boylston Street
Sixth Floor
Boston, MA 02116
(617) 727-1960

Department of Public Health
Division of Drug Rehabilitation
600 Washington Street
Boston, MA 02114
(617) 727-8617

MICHIGAN
Department of Public Health
Office of Substance Abuse Services
3500 North Logan Street
P.O. Box 30035
Lansing, MI 48909
(517) 373-8603

MINNESOTA
Department of Public Welfare
Chemical Dependency Program
    Division
Centennial Building
658 Cedar Street
4th Floor
Saint Paul, MN 55155
(612) 296-4614

MISSISSIPPI
Department of Mental Health
Division of Alcohol and Drug Abuse
1102 Robert E. Lee Building
Jackson, MS 39201
(601) 359-1297

MISSOURI
Department of Mental Health
Division of Alcoholism and Drug
    Abuse
2002 Missouri Boulevard
P.O. Box 687
Jefferson City, MO 65102
(314) 751-4942

MONTANA
Department of Institutions
Alcohol and Drug Abuse Division
1539 11th Avenue
Helena, MT 59620
(406) 449-2827

NEBRASKA
Department of Public Institutions
Division of Alcoholism and Drug Abuse
801 West Van Dorn Street
P.O. Box 94728
Lincoln, NB 68509
(402) 471-2851, Ext. 415

NEVADA
Department of Human Resources
Bureau of Alcohol and Drug Abuse
505 East King Street
Carson City, NV 89710
(702) 885-4790

NEW HAMPSHIRE
Department of Health and Welfare
Office of Alcohol and Drug Abuse
   Prevention
Hazen Drive
Health and Welfare Building
Concord, NH 03301
(603) 271-4627

NEW JERSEY
Department of Health
Division of Alcoholism
129 East Hanover Street CN 362
Trenton, NJ 08625
(609) 292-8949

Department of Health
Division of Narcotic and Drug Abuse
   Control
129 East Hanover Street CN 362
Trenton, NJ 08625
(609) 292-8949

NEW MEXICO
Health and Environment Department
Behavioral Services Division
Substance Abuse Bureau
725 Saint Michaels Drive
P.O. Box 968
Santa Fe, NM 87503
(505) 984-0020, Ext. 304

NEW YORK
Division of Alcoholism and Alcohol
   Abuse
194 Washington Avenue
Albany, NY 12210
(518) 474-5417

Division of Substance Abuse
   Services
Executive Park South
Box 8200
Albany, NY 12203
(518) 457-7629

NORTH CAROLINA
Department of Human Resources
Division of Mental Health, Mental
   Retardation and Substance Abuse
   Services
Alcohol and Drug Abuse Services
325 North Salisbury Street
Albemarle Building
Raleigh, NC 27611
(919) 733-4670

NORTH DAKOTA
Department of Human Services
Division of Alcoholism and Drug
   Abuse
State Capitol Building
Bismarck, ND 58505
(701) 224-2767

OHIO
Department of Health
Division of Alcoholism
246 North High Street
P.O. Box 118
Columbus, OH 43216
(614) 466-3543

Department of Mental Health
Bureau of Drug Abuse
65 South Front Street
Columbus, OH 43215
(614) 466-9023

OKLAHOMA
Department of Mental Health
Alcohol and Drug Programs
4545 North Lincoln Boulevard
Suite 100 East Terrace
P.O. Box 53277
Oklahoma City, OK 73152
(405) 521-0044

OREGON
Department of Human Resources
Mental Health Division
Office of Programs for Alcohol and
    Drug Problems
2575 Bittern Street, NE
Salem, OR 97310
(503) 378-2163

PENNSYLVANIA
Department of Health
Office of Drug and Alcohol
    Programs
Commonwealth and Forster Avenues
Health and Welfare Building
P.O. Box 90
Harrisburg, PA 17108
(717) 787-9857

RHODE ISLAND
Department of Mental Health,
    Mental Retardation and Hospitals
Division of Substance Abuse
Substance Abuse Administration
    Building
Cranston, RI 02920
(401) 464-2091

SOUTH CAROLINA
Commission on Alcohol and Drug
    Abuse
3700 Forest Drive
Columbia, SC 29204
(803) 758-2521

SOUTH DAKOTA
Department of Health
Division of Alcohol and Drug Abuse
523 East Capitol, Joe Foss Building
Pierre, SD 57501
(605) 773-4806

TENNESSEE
Department of Mental Health and
    Mental Retardation
Alcohol and Drug Abuse Services
505 Deaderick Street
James K. Polk Building, Fourth Floor
Nashville, TN 37219
(615) 741-1921

TEXAS
Commission on Alcoholism
809 Sam Houston State Office Building
Austin, TX 78701
(512) 475-2577

Department of Community Affairs
Drug Abuse Prevention Division
2015 South Interstate Highway 35
P.O. Box 13166
Austin, TX 78711
(512) 443-4100

UTAH
Department of Social Services
Division of Alcoholism and Drugs
150 West North Temple
Suite 350
P.O. Box 2500
Salt Lake City, UT 84110
(801) 533-6532

VERMONT
Agency of Human Services
Department of Social and
    Rehabilitation Services
Alcohol and Drug Abuse Division
103 South Main Street
Waterbury, VT 05676
(802) 241-2170

VIRGINIA
Department of Mental Health and
  Mental Retardation
Division of Substance Abuse
109 Governor Street
P.O. Box 1797
Richmond, VA 23214
(804) 786-5313

WASHINGTON
Department of Social and Health
  Service
Bureau of Alcohol and Substance
  Abuse
Office Building—44 W
Olympia, WA 98504
(206) 753-5866

WEST VIRGINIA
Department of Health
Office of Behavioral Health Services
Division on Alcoholism and Drug
  Abuse
1800 Washington Street East
Building 3 Room 451
Charleston, WV 25305
(304) 348-2276

WISCONSIN
Department of Health and Social
  Services
Division of Community Services
Bureau of Community Programs
Alcohol and Other Drug Abuse
  Program Office
1 West Wilson Street
P.O. Box 7851
Madison, WI 53707
(608) 266-2717

WYOMING
Alcohol and Drug Abuse Programs
Hathaway Building
Cheyenne, WY 82002
(307) 777-7115, Ext. 7118

GUAM
Mental Health & Substance Abuse
  Agency
P.O. Box 20999
Guam 96921

PUERTO RICO
Department of Addiction Control
  Services
Alcohol Abuse Programs
P.O. Box B-Y Rio Piedras Station
Rio Piedras, PR 00928
(809) 763-5014

Department of Addiction Control
  Services
Drug Abuse Programs
P.O. Box B-Y Rio Piedras Station
Rio Piedras, PR 00928
(809) 764-8140

VIRGIN ISLANDS
Division of Mental Health,
  Alcoholism & Drug Dependency
  Services
P.O. Box 7329
Saint Thomas, Virgin Islands 00801
(809) 774-7265

AMERICAN SAMOA
LBJ Tropical Medical Center
Department of Mental Health Clinic
Pago Pago, American Samoa 96799

TRUST TERRITORIES
Director of Health Services
Office of the High Commissioner
Saipan, Trust Territories 96950

Further Reading

Ainsworth, G. C. *Introduction to the History of Mycology*. Cambridge: Cambridge University Press, 1975.

Christensen, Clyde M. *The Molds and Man: An Introduction to the Fungi*. Minneapolis: University of Minnesota Press, 1965.

Cooke, R. C. *Fungi, Man and his Environment*. London: Longman, 1977.

Estrada, Alvaro. *Maria Sabina: Her Life and Chants*. trans. by Henry Munn. Santa Barbara, California: Ross-Erikson, 1981.

Furst, Peter T. *Hallucinogens and Culture*. San Francisco: Chandler and Sharp, 1976.

Guzmán, Gastón. *The Genus Psilocybe*. Vaduz: J. Cramer/A.R. Ganter, 1983.

Kibby, Geoffrey. *Mushrooms and Toadstools*. Oxford: Oxford University Press, 1979.

Lincoff, Gary and Mitchel, D. H., M.D. *Toxic and Hallucinogenic Mushroom Poisoning*. New York: Van Nostrand Reinhold, 1977.

Ott, Jonathan. "Recreational Use of Hallucinogenic Mushrooms in the United States." In: *Mushroom Poisoning: Treatment and Diagnosis*, Barry H. Rumack, M.D. and Emanuel Salsmen, M.D., eds. West Palm Beach, Florida: CRC Press, 1978.

Ross, Ian K. *Biology of the Fungi*. New York: McGraw-Hill, 1979.

Schultes, Richard Evans and Hofmann, Albert. *Plants of the Gods*. New York: McGraw-Hill, 1979.

Wasson, R. Gordon. *The Wondrous Mushroom: Mycolatry in Mesoamerica*. New York: McGraw-Hill, 1980.

Glossary

addiction   a condition caused by repeated drug use, including a compulsive urge to continue using the drug, a tendency to increase the dosage, and physiological and/or psychological dependence

alkaloids   any chemical containing nitrogen, carbon, hydrogen, and oxygen, usually occurring in plants

amino acid   an organic chemical compound that is the building block of proteins

analgesic   a drug that produces an insensitivity to pain without loss of consciousness

antibiotic   a substance produced by bacteria or fungi that when diluted is used to inhibit the growth of or kill another organism

carbohydrate   a compound composed of carbon, hydrogen, and oxygen, including sugar, starch, and cellulose

chlorophyll   the green coloring in plants essential to photosynthesis

curandero   an American Indian shaman who specializes in curing

Datura   a genus of widely distributed, strong-scented herbs, shrubs, or trees, including jimsonweed

earthstar   a fungus that resembles a star

fly agaric   the brightly colored hallucinogenic mushroom *Amanita muscaria* naturally found in Eurasia

fungus   any organism that lacks chlorophyll, is parasitic and/or saprophytic, exhibits distinct sexual and asexual phases, and reproduces from spores; includes mushrooms, molds, yeasts, bacteria, mildews, and toadstools

genus   a taxonomic category between family and species, comprised of related species, e.g., the fly agaric is a member of the genus *Amanita*

hallucinogen   a drug that produces a sensory impression that has no basis in external stimulation

hyphae   fine, cotton-like threads produced by the spores of fungi; dense tangles of hyphae form the mycelium *ibotenic acid*   a psychoactive compound which, together with muscimol, is the active ingredient in the major class of hallucinogenic mushrooms that includes the fly agaric

inert   any substance that does not have or manifest active properties when in contact with another substance and therefore does not produce any effects

jimsonweed   a poisonous annual weed of the genus *Datura* that produces prickly fruits and white or violet trumpet-shaped flowers

LSD   lysergic acid diethylamide; a hallucinogenic derived from a fungus that grows on rye or from morning-glory seeds

Mesoamerica   the region extending from north central North America to Nicaragua, including Mexico and the countries of Central America

metabolize   to convert, by using enzymes, one substance to compounds that can be readily eliminated from the body

morning glory   the plant *Turbina corymbosa* whose blue-and-white variety produces seeds which contain lysergic acid amide, a hallucinogenic related to LSD

muscimol   an unsaturated hydroxamic acid that, together with ibotenic acid, is the major hallucinogenic ingredient of the class of mushrooms that includes the fly agaric

mycelium   a subsurface fungal colony, composed of a tangle of hyphae, from which the actual mushrooms sprout and surface

mycologist   a specialist in the branch of botany dealing with fungi

mycorrhiza   a symbiotic relationship between a fungus and a seed plant, in which the fungal hypnae form an interwoven mass around the plant's rootlets, through which the fungus receives carbohydrates and the seed plant receives nitrogen, phosphorous, or potassium

neurotransmitter   a chemical, such as serotonin, that travels from the axon of one neuron, across the synaptic gap, and to the receptor site on the dendrite of an adjacent neuron, thus allowing communication between neural cells

ololiuqui   the vine *Rivea corymbosa* of the family Convolvulaceae that produces seeds which contain psychoactive agents similar to LSD

order   a category of taxonomic classification above the family and below the class

organic   derived from a living organism and containing carbon and hydrogen

parasite   an organism living in or on another organism, obtaining from it all or part of its nutritional requirements, and sometimes causing damage to the host

partial veil   the membrane that protects a mushroom's fragile gills and bursts as the cap begins to flatten out, leaving remnants on the mature stalk

PCP   phencyclidine; a drug first used as an anesthetic but later discontinued because of its adverse side effects; today abused for its stimulant, depressant, and/or hallucinogenic effects

peyote   a cactus that contains mescaline, a hallucinogenic drug, and is used legally by certain American Indians for religious and medical purposes

phalloidin   one of the two principal phallotoxins in *A. phalloides* that destroys the tissues of the liver and kidney

phallotoxins   toxins from the poisonous mushrooms that produce light to severe gastrointestinal distress, diarrhea, convulsive vomiting, and/or death

photosynthesis   the process by which a green plant uses sunlight to produce carbohydrates from carbon dioxide and water

physiological   related to the processes, activities, and phenomena characteristic of living organisms

psilocin   an unstable ingredient, related to the neurotransmitter serotonin, found in *Psilocybe*

Psilocybe   the genus of psychoactive mushrooms that contain the active ingredients psilocin and psilocybin

psilocybin   an acidic phosphoric acid ester of 4-hydroxymethyltryptamine, related to serotonin, and a psychoative ingredient in *Psilocybe*

psychedelic   producing hallucinations or having mind-altering or mind-expanding properties

psychoactive   altering mood and/or behavior

psychopharmacological related to a branch of pharmacology concerned with drugs that affect behavior or the subjective experience

puffball a basidiomycetous fungus that has a globe-like shape, produces a cloud of spores when pressed or struck, and is often edible

saprophyte an organism acquiring its necessary nutrients from dead or decaying organic matter

sclerotium a compact mass of hardened mycelium that contains reserve nutrients and remains dormant until favorable conditions occur that elicit the growth of hydrae or the production of spores

serotonin a neurotransmitter, similar to psilocybin and psilocin

somatic vegetative reproduction asexual reproduction, which does not involve the production of gametes, such as sperm or eggs, and is used by many basidiomycetous fungi

stinkhorn a foul-smelling basidiomycetous fungus of the order Phallales, such as *Phallus impudicus*, formerly used in preparing a salve for rheumatism

substrate the base on which an organism lives, e.g., soil is the substrate of most seed plants

symbiosis a relationship between two organisms whereby each individual benefits from the presence of the other; e.g., mycorrhiza is the symbiotic relationship between fungi and higher plants

sympathetic nervous system a system of nerves which, during an emergency, elicits responses of alertness, excitement, and alarm, and controls the expenditure of necessary energy

synthesize to create a chemical compound by combining elements or simpler compounds or by degrading a complex compound; generally refers to a laboratory process

taxonomy the orderly classification of living organisms according to their natural relationships and similarities

teponaztli a horizontal wooden drum used by Mexican Indians and made from a hollow log into which H-shaped slits have been cut

universal veil the thick membrane which, in the early developmental stages, envelops the fruit body of some mushrooms, such as the fly agaric; persists as the volva or as white "warts" on the caps of some mature varieties

velada   the mushroom vigil practiced by the Mazatec Indians of Mesoamerica

volva   the well-defined, jagged-edged cup which is formed after the universal veil breaks and from which the fruit body of such mushrooms as *A. phalloides*, *A. virosa*, and *A. verna* appear to grow.

Index

Peter E. Furst, Ph.D., is a professor of anthropology at the State University of New York (SUNY) at Albany and a research associate in ethnobotany at the Botanical Museum of Harvard University.

Solomon H. Snyder, M.D., is Distinguished Service Professor of Neuroscience, Pharmacology and Psychiatry at The Johns Hopkins University School of Medicine. He has served as president of the Society for Neuroscience and in 1978 received the Albert Laster Award in Medical Research. He has authored *Uses of Marijuana, Madness and the Brain, The Troubled Mind, Biological Aspects of Mental Disorder,* and edited *Perspective in Neuropharmacology: A Tribute to Julius Axelrod.* Professor Snyder was a research associate with Dr. Axelrod at the National Institute of Health.

Barry L. Jacobs, Ph.D., is currently a professor in the program of neuroscience at Princeton University. Professor Jacobs is author of *Serotonin Neurotransmission and Behavior* and *Hallucinogens: Neurochemical, Behavioral and Clinical Perspectives.* He has written many journal articles in the field of neuroscience and contributed numerous chapters to books on behavior and brain science. He has been a member of several panels of the National Institute of Mental Health.

Jerome H. Jaffe, M.D., formerly professor of psychiatry at the College of Physicians and Surgeons, Columbia University, has been named recently Director of the Addiction Research Center of the National Institute on Drug Abuse. Dr. Jaffe is also a psychopharmacologist and has conducted research on a wide range of addictive drugs and developed treatment programs for addicts. He has acted as Special Consultant to the President on Narcotics and Dangerous Drugs and was the first director of the White House Special Action Office for Drug Abuse Prevention.